HENRY FIELDING'S
TOM JONES

GROVER CRONIN, JR.
PROFESSOR OF ENGLISH
FORDHAM UNIVERSITY

MONARCH PRESS
A DIVISION OF SIMON & SCHUSTER, INC.
1 WEST 39th STREET
NEW YORK, NEW YORK 10018

Printed in the United States of America.

Standard Book Number: 671-00614-2
Library of Congress Catalog Card Number: 65-7304

CONTENTS

INTRODUCTION

England in the eighteenth century was still an agricultural nation. The Industrial Revolution was beginning, but the beginnings were comparatively slow. The British Empire was steadily growing, and with it inevitably grew finance and commerce. Seaports like Bristol became increasingly important in the shaping of British economy.

Despite all of the unmistakable omens of change, England remained through the century pre-eminently rural in its complexion. Land remained the most "respectable" source of wealth and very much the outstanding status symbol. Even the representatives of the future, of the new order—the bankers, investors, merchants—were anxious, as their fortunes grew, to emulate older ways, to buy country seats and ape the manners of the established aristocracy.

Wealth, however obtained, was, in the eighteenth century, concentrated in the hands of a comparative few. Individuals had their ups and downs; the general economy wavered as it always does in periods of little or no regulatory control. In general, however, those singularly favored by birth, native intelligence, and circumstance were able to add impressively to their fortunes or even to emerge from humble backgrounds and amass extraordinary fortunes. The eighteenth century was a golden age in the building of the stately homes of England. Architecture became a mania and men vied with one another in the creation of magnificent estates—estates comprising thousands, sometimes hundreds of thousands of acres, and elaborate homes of hundreds and hundreds of rooms. Although this kind of ostentation was never the prerogative of more than a very, very small percentage of the population, throughout the century an increasing number of men were able to enter the frantic contest in domestic and landscape architecture. Thus, in another way, we see the old order changing. There were the ancient families, safe, solid, established landowners (often affected by the craze for display in spite of their inherited privileges, sense of position, and contempt for the parvenus); there were also the successful invaders of the sacrosanct precincts of the privileged.

THE CLASSES OF SOCIETY. England has long had a monarchical form of government. For a few years in the seventeenth century it experimented, under Oliver Cromwell, with a Commonwealth, but in 1660 Charles II returned to his hereditary throne and the succession has been unbroken. At the apex of the social structure, then, is the King (or Queen) and the Royal Family. Next, at least in theoretical social importance, is the Nobility, those who enjoy titles and honors conferred by their sovereign, titles and honors that are (or were) usually hereditary: Dukes, Marquises, Viscounts, Earls, and Barons—all addressed, at least informally, as "Lord." Next come the Knights, the higher class of whom hold the rank of Baronet (not to be confused with a Barony). Knights are addressed as "Sir." Then there are the untitled but substantial landholders, the so-called landed gentry. Sometimes representative of the nobility, the knighthood, or the landed gentry—and sometimes not—are the men prominent in public life as professional men, politicians, financiers, and the like. Next proceed the tradesmen, some of them men of comfortable means but not quite welcome in the brilliant eighteenth-century world of wit and fashion. Of comparable stature to the tradesmen were the countrymen whose landholdings were modest, at least compared to those of their neighbors who owned hundreds and thousands of acres. At the bottom of the social ladder were the laborers, but even within this class were scrupulously defined (if not always observed) distinctions. An artisan, for example, a skilled carpenter or ironworker or mason, was a considerable cut above an unskilled worker such as a bargeman or a porter.

THEORY AND PRACTICE. The hierarchical structure of eighteenth-century English society sometimes misleads modern readers into imagining that life proceeded in a completely orderly way. Nothing could be further from the truth. Although in the "best society" a certain deference was often shown by one of lower rank to one of higher rank, in the give and take of everyday life considerable freedom was taken, and this was actually expected. Lords subjected to the scurrilous abuse of fishwives were rarely surprised; wealthy bankers were inclined to be contemptuous of the follies and vices of young men of family who were demonstrably headed for Debtors' Prison. Looking at the problem from another point of view, girls of humble origins were not infrequently courted by men of much higher station than they were, and fathers of birth and breeding were not averse to the crossing of social lines, especially if such crossing might bring financial advantage.

SOCIETY AND RELIGION. There were few professions an educated gentleman could hope to enter in the eighteenth century. That of churchman was one of the most available. It was available to the sons, especially the younger sons, of the most powerful lords of the land; it was also available to bright young men with few or no family connections. The Church was an avenue to fame, social prominence, worldly comfort.

It must not be thought, however, that the English Church of the eighteenth century was utterly venal. It had its brilliant thinkers and its good men. Not all who sought a career in the Church did so with an eye to material advantage. But many students of the eighteenth century have detected a kind of torpor in the Church, an absence of spirituality. And if generalizations about the religious climate of a particular age must always be peculiarly dubious, requiring, as they do, more rigorous scientific methods than earlier historians possessed and a first-hand acquaintance with evidence such as we can never hope to possess, there is no doubt but what a fair number of Englishmen took Holy Orders because it was the expedient thing to do.

The Church of England was not without rivals. Born of the Reformation spirit, more specifically of Henry VIII's resentment of Rome's intransigence, ultimately given diplomatic shape by the administrative genius of Elizabeth I, the Church of England was a State church, an "established" religion, the only officially "recognized" religion in the country. The Church of England, astutely and diplomatically, attempted to follow a "middle way" (*via media*) between traditional Catholic teaching and the doctrines of the new "Reformers" like Martin Luther. Unavoidably it offended many people: traditionalists, even those traditionalists who were professedly loyal to Elizabeth and the State, and the more extreme Reformers. The battle that brought on the death of Charles I, the suspension of monarchical government, and the savageries of the seventeenth century was brewing during the reign of Elizabeth, came to a boil during the reign of Charles I (and cost him his head), and only seemed to simmer down during the reign of Charles II and his successors. The old animosities persisted.
The Established Church (Church of England) thus found itself in a *favored* position in the eighteenth century, but it was also a beleaguered Church. It tried, on the one hand, to accommodate itself to its age, to be a "polite," an "enlightened" Church—and by doing so sacrificed Apostolic zeal. On the other hand it tried to suppress dissent, but found itself without the means to do so. It was, in effect, a Church in a quandary. It had an educated clergy, had the support of the State, but it faced problems it was not equipped to handle.

It also had a clergy that was educated but not always entirely motivated by the highest spiritual motives. It was a well-known fact that if a man took Holy Orders and played his cards right, he could cut a figure in the fashionable world. The literature of the eighteenth century suggests that many who were not zealots or professional satirists were more than a little worried by the behavior and attitudes of the clergy of the Church.

There is something not a little bit curious in the fact that many who were disturbed by the way things were going in the Established Church were equally disturbed by all corrective measures. In part, this is a part of the anti-clericalism that was generated by: a) the scandalous wars of religion of the seventeenth century; b) the new awareness of the possibilities of controlled scientific experiment; c) a hope that men of good will could learn to live in peace with one another without disputes on dogma. This hopeful faith in the possibility of formulating a set of doctrines all men could live by was called *Deism* or *The Religion of Nature*. It attracted the attention and won the allegiance of some of the best minds of the eighteenth century.

Deism, however, was radical. In the interests of peace, civil and intellectual, it was willing to throw overboard many of the most sacred dogmas of the Christian revelation. English Dissent, therefore, must be seen not only as a protest against the lethargy of the English Church but also a protest against what were looked upon as abstract philosophical challenges to traditional Christianity.

Unquestionably one of the greatest figures in the history of English religion is John Wesley (1703-1791), founder of the sect that came to be known as the Methodists. Wesley had no intention of becoming a "heretic." He was for years a devout member of the Church of England, but while at Oxford he came to believe that religious practices had become too tepid, that the Church had become too wordly, too comfortable, smug, complacent; he, with his younger brother, Charles, attempted to start a religious revival. There was initial success; but indifference, contempt, and utter hostility hardened him in his original convictions and gradually drove him to separation from the Established Church and to the formation of a new sect, the so-called Methodists. The Wesley brothers had a great deal to do with the ultimate overthrow of the old social patterns of England. The so-called "upper-classes" despised the Wesleys; the common people loved them, adopted their teachings, and, years later, triumphed.

Other dissenting sects are obviously important. The Quakers, for example, with their insistence on nonviolence and the sacredness of one's "inner light," contributed much to the religious sophistication of the period. They, like the Methodists, were, predictably, subjected to ridicule, but, whatever satirists, even thoroughly admirable satirists like Fielding, have to say about them, they have made a permanent imprint on the English consciousness.

The Unitarians of the eighteenth century seemed especially dangerous in that they denied the central doctrine of the Trinity. But in their boldness they were essentially allying themselves with the deistic spirit of their age, and they were posing to all religious thinkers problems of the greatest importance. Their contribution to the intellectual—and religious—history of the eighteenth century must never be under-emphasized. One must never think of Deism alone; one must also recall the ideas of the Unitarians.

Although the Roman Catholics have been for centuries looked upon as one of the most dangerous enemies of the Established Church, they scarcely rank among the properly so-called "Dissenting" sects. In the first place, they are members of the Church originally dissented from; in the second place, they disagree with the libertarian principles of biblical interpretation that justify the dissenting sects; in the third place, they belonged to a rival religion of such power and such authority that they were more feared than were members of newer "dissenting" sects and, with a few exceptions, were subjected to greater legal disabilities. In spite of the fact that the Catholic Church was feared, hated, and legislated against (indeed, was outlawed) in the eighteenth century, it continued its missionary work to restore England to the Roman communion and thus played a part, even if a disruptive and disturbing part, in the religious history of the English eighteenth century.

EDUCATION. The changing patterns of eighteenth-century social life are reflected in the changing patterns of eighteenth-century education. On the whole, so far as the intellectual history of the age is concerned, the old classical patterns prevailed. On the other hand, obligations to respond to the new needs of a changing society were gradually recognized.

THE OLD PATTERNS. Traditional education in the eighteenth century was rigidly classical, at least so far as boys were concerned. Shortly after learning how to read and write, a boy was introduced into an educational system in which he would find himself saturated with Latin and Greek literature. Little else was, officially, considered to be of importance. Obviously boys were given some instruction in a few practical subjects—arithmetic, for example, or geography—but the curriculum was remorselessly "literary" or rhetorical. There were authors all educated men were expected to know: Homer, Virgil, Horace, Juvenal, to mention only a few. The system made for a means of sophisticated communication that seems utterly unimaginable in the twentieth-century world. It had its weaknesses; it had its strengths. It ignored much that we think important; it emphasized much that is important that we ignore.

Training in elementary subjects was given in various ways: by private tutors, by men or women who earned a precarious living conducting little local private schools. Formal education really began when a young man entered either a Public School or a local Grammar School.

The English Public Schools are those endowed schools (by public benefactors or benefactresses) intended to benefit the entire nation. Many have become well-known names throughout the globe: Eton, Harrow, Winchester, Westminister, Rugby—and dozens of comparable merit. They resemble—perhaps it would be more felicitous to say that they are the models of—our American expensive private preparatory schools.

Although they were designed to give an essentially aristocratic education (i.e., one devised to make an eighteenth-century English gentleman rather than a man with special skills), they seem to have been rather surprisingly democratic. Many of the students in the public schools were sons of lords and gentry; many were also sons of men of comparatively modest circumstances. Horace Walpole, son of the Prime Minister of England, of an extraordinarily wealthy man, of one of the most powerful politicians in English history, attended Eton, as did many of the sons of influential parents. At Eton, however, one of his closest friends was Thomas Gray, destined to become famous as the author of the *Elegy in a Country Churchyard,* whose family circumstances were straitened indeed. The very rich and those of modest means rubbed elbows in the English public schools to a surprising extent.

Even boys who, for one reason or another, could not attend one of the famous public schools, had good educational opportunities. Throughout England there were many so-called grammar schools—schools that taught the rudiments of Latin grammar and trained boys in the close reading of the best-known Latin authors.

In curriculum there was little to distinguish the public schools from the grammar schools; both types of school prepared young men for entrance into a university. Not only the curriculum but also the quality of the instruction was about equal in both types of school. Samuel Johnson, for example, testifies to the solidity of the education he received at Lichfield Grammar School.

There were two English universities in the eighteenth century: Oxford and Cambridge. It is often alleged that they were intellectually stagnant; there is no doubt that they made few demands on those students who were disinclined to work, and there is no doubt that many men sought academic posts only to form acquaintances that might be able to advance them to lucrative positions in the Church. But there is also reason to believe that the universities were not so bad as they are said to have been. When one examines lists of eighteenth-century graduates of Oxford and Cambridge, one quickly learns that an impressive number of brilliant men were at the universities during this maligned period.

THE GRAND TOUR. At the universities as well as at the schools, rich and poor rubbed elbows. After leaving the university (sometimes without troubling to take a degree), a prosperous young man customarily made an extended, leisurely tour of the Continent and thus rounded out his education and prepared himself for entrance into the great world, the world of wit and fashion.

CONVERSATION. The entire educational system had a single purpose: the formation of a gentleman, and a gentleman was, in a manner of speaking, his own excuse for being. He might become a great statesman or an outstanding clergyman, a jurist, a scientist, a painter; but this was incidental. Education as such made him a man acceptable in polite drawing-rooms where he could enjoy the clash of ideas and epigrams, and talk about the vital issues of the day. Education can almost be said to exist to make civilized conversation possible. Looking at the picture from another vantagepoint, however, it can also be said that conversation was an integral part of the educational process. It carried on where the universities left off. Every man has his idiosyncrasies, his areas of ignorance, his prejudices. In theory, conversation helped a man to rid himself of his limitations.

UTILITARIAN ASPECTS OF EDUCATION. Although the ideal was the formation of a gentleman, in practice many young men went up to the university with more pragmatic ends in view. Very many, for example, entered the Church and hoped through their associations to fall into choice ecclesiastical benefices and thus be able to claim right of entrance into the alluring society from which they were often barred by reason of their lower-class origins.

THE NEW PATTERNS. One feature of the eighteenth century that immediately impresses the observer is its remarkable sense of permanence. It would seem that nearly everyone in the century thought that the ways of the world had been immutably set, that things would go on as they were pretty much forever. In spite of this delusive sense of permanence, everything in eighteenth-century England was changing and changing rapidly. Some changes have already been indicated: the growth of the mercantile class and the ferment in religion. Perhaps the single most important fact in the history of the century was the rise of the middle-class.

This fact was to some extent imperceptible because there was a predictable assimilation by the middle-class of the manners and attitudes of the old aristocracy. But for every tradesman who fought his way to the kind of wealth that enabled him to build or buy a great estate in the country, keep a town house, engage a large staff of servants, have the luxury of his own coach, and find acceptance in the most exclusive social circles, there were hundreds whose industry brought them a measure of comfort but not the external symbols of unmistakable success. Some of them in planning the education of their sons conformed to the old patterns but an increasing number demanded a more practical, utilitarian kind of education—one that would communicate those skills that led to money. Side by side with the old aristocratic idealism (to which lip service was sometimes paid by hard-headed businessmen with larceny in their hearts) was a new, frank emphasis on a relationship between education and everyday life.

Even among conservative educators there was a willingness to question established methods. Should education be as exclusively literary as it had been or should cognizance be taken of the new science? Should a boy be browbeaten into a knowledge of Latin and Greek or should he be persuaded that these studies have a genuine relevance to his life?

THE TOWN. It has been remarked that eighteenth-century England was predominantly agricultural. It was, in other words, made up of vast stretches of land, much of it under cultivation of tenant farmers (farmers who paid rent to the great landowners—the "squires"—who had title to the property, much of it worked by independent farmers whose holdings were modest and whose profits were chancy.) It was a nation of small villages, connected with one another by unbelievably bad roads. There were many towns, useful as outlets for the products of the farms and as places where country people could go for various services—legal, medical, and the like. There were also cities, and the cities grew in importance as the century went on. But in a very real sense there was only one city: London. This was *The Town.* (The "city" of London is only one small part of it, the financial district. When one speaks of "the city," one intends what Americans mean when they say "Wall Street.") London was utterly different from all of the rest of England, and was, accordingly, eyed with suspicion by a fair number of people in the rest of England, especially those whose situation made it unlikely that they would ever visit that vast and sprawling center of all folly, affectation, and vice.

London was the civilized world. A man might have ten thousand acres in Lancashire or Yorkshire, but if he had any desire to shine in the world, he had to spend a certain amount of time each year in London.

If London was the civilized world, it was also (as its detractors darkly suggested) a sink of iniquity. This should not be surprising; the eighteenth century obviously had no monopoly on sin. Nor can anyone now think it likely that sin then would have been confined to any particular social class. What startles the modern reader is the excessive dirtiness of this particular sink of iniquity. The streets were narrow and dirty. The buildings were crowded together and were often mere hovels. The shops, especially those purveying food, were dirty. Putting it succinctly, the eighteenth century was a civilized age, a polite age, and a remarkably unsanitary age.

THE SINS OF LONDON. It is improbable that any reader needs a catalogue of the favorite sins of this city and of this particular age. They were the sins that have proved perennially popular. A few features of eighteenth-century London may, however, be emphasized for the benefit of the modern reader.

1. Poverty was so widespread and so terrible that thousands of girls were literally forced into prostitution. It may well be that a statistical examination of this social problem in this century would not prove particularly sensational, but the historian can

scarcely ignore the curious flagrancy of this species of vice at that time. And the contrast between the "politeness" of the age and the utter degradation behind the facade of politeness is startling. One must always remember that the century was not only the century of the moral Johnson but also the century of the libertine Boswell.

2. Gambling. Once again, it should not be surprising that gambling was popular in Fielding's England. It can, however, be said that among the so-called upper classes, gambling was almost compulsive and frenetic. Extraordinary amounts were wagered, horrifying debts were contracted, careers were ruined and lives were destroyed.

3. Drinking. This vice is also directly related to the existence of intolerable poverty. Spirits, particularly gin, were cheap (from our point of view, unimaginably cheap) and one could be "dead drunk for a penny." Understandably, large numbers sought oblivion from the anguishes of life—the pangs of hunger, endless toil—, and the horrifying consequences have been recorded for all time by that matchless artist, William Hogarth (1697-1764), in his print entitled "Gin Lane."

   It goes without saying that the abjectly poor were not the only ones who drank to excess. Not a few members of the more privileged classes were notorious for their intemperance. And their intemperance was peculiarly offensive because it often led to gross violations of human rights. Poor itinerant street musicians, for example, would be summoned to entertain fashionable roisterers in a private room of a tavern—only, later, to be kicked downstairs for their services and pains.

SPORT IN EIGHTEENTH-CENTURY ENGLAND. With reference to *Tom Jones,* only a few of the most popular eighteenth-century sports need be mentioned. One of these is fox-hunting, often referred to merely as "hunting." In the English view, hunting is a sport that is played on horseback; if one goes after game afoot, the sport is denominated "shooting."

Property rights in the eighteenth century were jealously guarded. It was illegal to hunt or shoot in another man's estate. Landowners as a matter of course had, among their servants, a gamekeeper, whose duty it was to preserve the game from "poachers."

Although only hunting and shooting play a part in *Tom Jones,* the reader of the novel should be aware of the fact that sport had by Fielding's time become a most important part of the English way of life. The English had begun to play cricket, to take up sailing and rowing. They were also still interested in sports that we tend to look upon as brutal, such as bearbaiting and cock-fighting.

SUMMARY. This introduction has been designed as an introduction to the lusty, brawling age depicted in *Tom Jones.* It has been designed to alert the reader of Fielding's masterpiece to the contradictions within the age he so ably depicted. It has been designed to force the modern reader to face up to the obvious fact that Fielding is writing about an age that is shockingly different from all ages nearer to the modern reader's own time. When Fielding wrote, the Industrial Revolution was in its beginning. The labor movement had hardly begun; the conditions of labor were, from our point of view, incomprehensible. Modern science was still in its infancy; a man could be considered an educated man and not know a single thing about physics, chemistry, biology, or any of the other sciences that we assume are an essential part of the intellectual equipment of an educated man.

On the other hand, Fielding belonged to a changing age, a dramatically changing age. Whether Fielding was completely conscious of it or not, England was changing. Excitement was in the air. Questions were being asked, questions about philosophy, about theology, about educational theory, about everything that touched life. *Tom Jones* reflects the dynamism of its age.

The world described in *Tom Jones* is an utterly different world from that we know. On the other hand, Fielding was convinced that he was describing not only the customs and ways of life of his own time but also what he called human nature. His conviction deserves our careful consideration.

FIELDING'S LIFE

Born on April 22, 1707, at Sharpham Park in Somersetshire, Henry Fielding was destined to confront a peculiarly eighteenth-century problem: he was a gentleman by birth but he had no assured income. His father was an army officer of very limited means; his mother was the daughter of a distinguished jurist and inherited some property in Dorsetshire but she could scarcely be described as an heiress.

The distinction between a gentleman and a non-gentleman is difficult for the modern reader to understand. It is a distinction that was never clearly drawn. Essentially, Fielding's status derived from the fact that his family had kinship with nobility, were landowners, were educated. The Fieldings had a kind of inborn consciousness of belonging to the socially acceptable class.

Fielding was educated as a gentleman. He went to Eton when he was twelve years old, and remained there for seven years. At Eton he formed valuable friendships with men who were later to become famous, notably with William Pitt the elder who played so important a part in the establishment of the English in America and who was, in many other ways, one of the most prominent statesmen of his day. He also acquired at Eton a solid education. He discovered in himself a genuine passion for literature, and in his subsequent career showed that he is among the most literary of our authors. This does not mean that he is ever pretentious or pompous: it means that he shows, casually and gracefully, that he is an exceptionally well-read man—well-read in the classics, in English literature, in Continental literature. Fielding had a magnificent sense of humor and a remarkable talent for farce; it is, accordingly, often forgotten that he is an author with an impeccable literary education.

In the normal course of events, a young man leaving Eton would go up to one of the two English universities, Oxford or Cambridge. Fielding chose not to, for reasons that are not altogether clear. The reasons may have been related to the financial circumstances of his family. He was soon, however, persuaded to go on with his education, and went to the University of Leyden, in Holland, to study law.

He left Leyden in 1728 without taking a degree. It is likely that this interruption of his studies was prompted by the fact that he was short of funds. In any event, he settled down in London and began his professional career as a writer by contributing to the London stage.

Fielding is not much remembered as a dramatist. He was, however, a thoroughly respectable craftsman, and his work for the theater taught him much that he was later to use when he turned his hand to the novel.

His career as dramatist, however should not be looked upon only as preparation for his more famous career as novelist. Some of his plays, especially his farces, were remarkably successful. The first to please the town was his *Tom Thumb* (1730), a burlesque of contemporary tragedies and perhaps the most permanently significant of Fielding's writings for the stage.

Another farce that met with a gratifying reception was *Pasquin*, produced in 1736. And Fielding's most important play from the point of view of its effect on his career was *The Historical Register for 1737*. Both *Pasquin* and *The Historical Register* were satires directed at Sir Robert Walpole, the Prime Minister.

Whether the satires were wholly justified is a matter for historians to determine, and thus far opinions are divided. What is certain, however, is that Walpole was an aggressive, shrewd politician and, not surprisingly, made many enemies. Fielding allied himself with the anti-

Walpolians, the Opposition, and courageously contributed his pen to their cause.

Walpole may well have been a better man and truer patriot than his enemies made him out to be, but he was unquestionably ruthless in his political battles. As events turned out, *The Historical Register* was Fielding's final play. Stung by the gibes, Walpole pushed through Parliament a Licensing Act (1737) which made it necessary for a playwright to secure a license for his work before it could be produced. Fielding realized at once that he would never be able to have his satirical dramas licensed.

Walpole's vindictive gesture threatened not only Fielding's literary career but his entire livelihood. Always improvident, Fielding throughout his life faced financial crisis after financial crisis. In 1734 he climaxed a romantic courtship by eloping with his beloved Charlotte Cradock. She was not only beautiful but an heiress, and the lovers settled down in a country place in Dorsetshire, a county in which he had spent much of his boyhood and for which he had a special affection. It did not take him long to dissipate his wife's money; in less than a year he was forced to return to London and to work for the theatre. Somehow he had managed to preserve enough of Charlotte's fortune to purchase a controlling interest in a London theatre, and thus earned his living as a manager as well as a dramatist.

When Walpole's Licensing Act was passed, then, Fielding had a wife and two daughters to support—and the Act made it impossible for him to support them. But one of the most attractive features of Fielding is his resiliency, his indomitable spirit. Instead of moping and indulging in self-pity, he remembered his early interest in the law, enrolled in the Middle Temple (one of the ancient law schools of England), and soon qualified for admission to the bar.

allegories of a John Bunyan (of *Pilgrim's Progress* fame) or the highly Although Fielding had a genuine interest in and talent for the law, he had an irresistible vocation to literature and continued to support his family by his versatile pen. While carrying on his studies at the Middle Temple, for example, he was contributing essays to a periodical known as *The Champion,* essays that show the alertness of his mind and the depth of his concern with social issues. Fielding is a comic writer essentially; the reader is well advised to remember that some of the most profound observations of the human condition have been made by comic writers.

The most crucial event in Fielding's life was the publication in 1740 (the year in which he was admitted to the bar) of the first two volumes of a novel that was to prove to be a turning-point in the history of English literature: Samuel Richardson's *Pamela.* This is said to be the first modern novel—at least, the first modern novel in English. In its tightness of organization, in its penetrating studies of character, in its insistence on the prime importance of moral issues, it clearly marks a new development in prose narrative. Obviously Richardson owed much to his predecessors, but it is equally obvious that nothing quite like *Pamela* had hitherto been attempted in English.

The novel created a sensation. The plot was relatively simple. Pamela Andrews, the virtuous daughter of "poor but honest" parents, found domestic employment in the household of a young man whose mother had recently died. The young man, Mr. B——, is quick to notice the charms of the servant-girl and attempts to seduce her.

The story is mostly told in letters written by Pamela to relatives and friends. The device has the advantage of coherence; we see events almost entirely from Pamela's point of view. It has the obvious disadvantage of one-sidedness, and a skeptical reader may well indulge the suspicion that Pamela presents an excessively favorable view of her virtue.

The novel is insistently, perhaps too insistently, moral in tone. It was meant to entertain, but one feels that Richardson was more interested in being edifying than in being entertaining. And there is no evidence in his works that Richardson ever had any doubts about the value of his teaching.

Some readers in his time, however, and a fair number of readers of later times, have had misgivings. They feel: 1) that Richardson is prurient in his depiction of the many assaults made on Pamela's virtue, that the scenes are so graphic as to be in dubious taste; 2) that Richardson's ethical code is centered on sexual ethics almost to the exclusion of every other element in the philosophical and religious problem of what constitutes the good life; 3) that Pamela's jealously preserved virtue was preserved for shockingly practical reasons—to persuade the wealthy and socially acceptable Mr. B—— to marry her.

Fielding shared this skeptical attitude toward the moral worth of *Pamela.* In 1741 those contemporary readers who were not, as the saying goes, "taken in" by Richardson's sanctimonious heroine were delighted with a remarkably clever parody entitled *Shamela.* Fielding was probably the author. The book certainly represents his views and it also in style and spirit reminds us of his other writings. It is, in many respects, a ribald book, but behind the facade of ribaldry are deeply held and extremely important moral convictions. Although the satire is devastating, it is also good-humored. To this day it ranks among the great English parodies.

Hilarious and important as *Shamela* was, it was a mere jeu d'esprit, an enormously clever but comparatively slight joke, compared to Fielding's next answer to the challenge—moral and literary—presented by Richardson's success. In 1742 Fielding tried to show the world how a novel should be written; he published his *Joseph Andrews*.

In a sense *Joseph Andrews* continues the joke. Joseph is represented as the brother of Pamela. He, like his sister, finds his virtue sorely tried but overcomes his aggressors. Fielding confronts, even with comical characters and farcical situations, fundamentally serious moral problems.

It is clear, too, that Fielding is trying to show the English public that he is a better writer than Richardson. Although it is usually acknowledged that Richardson has many virtues as a writer, for example the dogged thoroughness with which he examines feelings and motives, the feeling that he has for the climate of his age, his skill in the fashioning of plot, and his management of suspense and surprise, it is also usually acknowledged that Richardson had limitations.

He was, for example, essentially a middle-class author and was not at home in other societies than those he knew. His success was in large part the result of his championing of the rising middle-class. Pamela was the pre-destined darling of shopgirls and chamber-maids.

Richardson, furthermore, compared with authors like Fielding, was ill-educated. He is, in some respects, greatly to be admired because he succeeded admirably well in training himself to be a much more than competent man of letters. But he never had the peculiar advantages of a public school education—nor even of a good grammar school education. The consequence of this was that one encounters little of grace and wit and urbanity in Richardson. His style is rather turgid, heavy. Fielding scintillates, dazzles, charms. He is full of clever allusions, apt quotations, rhetorical flourishes; Richardson is heavy-handed and more than somewhat dull. He compels our interest but he is scarcely a companionable author. Fielding is among the most companionable of all authors in our English literary history.

Although he was more often than not in straitened circumstances, Fielding was an aristocrat to his fingertips; he had assurance; he never hesitated to speak out against the middle-class pieties of his day.

On the other hand, Fielding was also a professional man of letters, sensitive to changes in taste, aware of the new demands of the public. He could not help but recognize the enormous popularity of Richardson and he instinctively knew that a new day had dawned. He decided to become a novelist.

He did not, however, propose to be a mere imitator of Richardson, for whose work he had scant respect. He obviously recognized the disadvantages of the epistolary novel, the story told by means of letters from the various characters to one another. The epistolary novel was destined to be a much imitated form, but Fielding (except in parody) would have nothing to do with it.

In his search for ways of achieving unity of plot, psychological depth in characterization, moral seriousness, and relevance to essential human nature and to the world as we know it, he summoned up his recollections of the literature that had nurtured his youth and had continued to solace his maturity: the classics. He decided that Homer and Virgil were far better models than was Richardson, and he elaborated his own theory of the novel as "a comic epic in prose."

He saw that prose was clearly the literary vehicle of the future. Prose had a long and noble history; prose romances had been written in ancient Greece; prose was the ordinary language of learning; much that was best in English literature was in prose. But there was also a well-entrenched feeling that in imaginative literature poetry had the edge over prose. Homer and Virgil, Chaucer, Shakespeare and Spenser, Milton, Pope and Dryden—these were the great names. One of the central tasks which the schools attempted—and which they had been attempting for centuries—was the training of the young in the efficacious reading of poetry. Of course, there were important prose writers: Herodotus, Thucydides, Demosthenes; Caesar and Cicero; Malory; Sir Philip Sidney; Swift and Defoe. But the traditionally educated man was pre-eminently qualified to bring a critical intelligence to bear upon poetry.

But a classical education had once been almost the only kind of education, and had been the prerogative of the privileged. By Fielding's day, everything was changing. Milliners' apprentices were learning how to read, and were reading. Sons of bargemen were looking forward to advancing themselves in life through training schools which taught rudiments—reading, writing, arithmetic, geography, and the like. Through the eighteen century the reading public grew and grew. Compared to earlier reading publics, it was undiscriminating. It was not equipped to appreciate the fine points of Pope's poetry. It could appreciate story, narratives about people they could recognize, narratives that had relevance to their own lives. The new readers did not want the religious allegories of a John Bunyan (of Pilgrim's Progress fame) or the highly allusive and intellectualized prose of Swift's *Gulliver's Travels*. And thus the modern English novel was born, though it is perhaps more accurate to say that the novel as a form has a kind of permanence, is always there, but meets the special needs of special audiences. At all events, Richardson and Fielding and many of their contemporaries recognized the inevitability of the novel in their own time, and the demand for the novel has not slackened since, nor does it seem likely to. We are not likely ever to turn away from our modern egalitarianism; education is never again likely to be exclusive. The novel has assumed many forms and will probably assume many, many more; its establishment as a dominant generic type is largely the achievement of Richardson and Fielding.

Although jocularly related to Pamela and more seriously (yet good-naturedly) antithetic to its style and spirit, *Joseph Andrews* must further be examined as Fielding's first professional encounter with what he recognized as a new way of writing, as his response to the needs and demands of a new audience.

Joseph Andrews is deservedly loved and admired. It should not be looked upon merely as a preparation for *Tom Jones,* nor should it be permitted to live in the shadow of *Tom Jones.* It is a great novel in its own right, but it lacks the subtlety, intricacy, and sheer massiveness of Fielding's best-known novel.

Immediately after *Joseph Andrews,* Fielding published, in 1743, *Jonathan Wild the Great,* in which, under the guise of writing about a highwayman, he returns to the attack on his old political foe, Sir Robert Walpole. Interesting from the point of view of Fielding's political stances, of his ethical philosophy, and of his strategy as satirist, *Jonathan Wild* is perhaps too topical to enjoy widespread popularity today.

Shortly before the appearance of *Jonathan Wild,* the dark years of Fielding's life began. In 1742 his health began to fail. In 1744 his wife and daughter died and he became, understandably, extremely despondent. His physical disabilities and emotional agonies were augmented by his still unresolved financial problems.

But Fielding was nothing if not courageous. He lived with instinctive grace, and it was during these years of torment that he produced the work that he will always be remembred for: *Tom Jones.* It was published on February 28, 1749—and was a great success.

One of these remarkable things about *Tom Jones* is that it was written when Fielding was involved in many other undertakings. He had passed the bar, and was appointed to a judicial position of considerable importance, that of Justice of the Peace for Westminster (a very important part of London) and later of Middlesex (another important part of London). He took his duties seriously, and he has a permanent place in English history not only as a man of letters but also as a jurist and social reformer—especially as a social reformer.

Four years after the death of Charlotte Cradock, he married a second wife, Mary Daniel, who had been a servant-girl in his household. By her he had two sons and a daughter; but the point to emphasize to students of the eighteenth century is that Fielding was not only a "born gentleman" but at the same time a man utterly devoid of social prejudices.

In his brave confrontation of life, Fielding remained active to the end. In 1751 he published his last novel, *Amelia,* which is, it must be admitted, little read today but which is generally considered to be one of the most thoughtful enunciations of his philosophical and social positions. After *Amelia* he contributed essays to a periodical, published twice weekly, called the *Covent-Garden Journal;* and anyone interested in Fielding's habits of mind and his opinions on such things as crime and punishment, on the problems raised by poverty and selfishness, and on the moral climate of his age, had best read the *Covent-Garden Journal.*

In 1754, racked by ill-health, Fielding and his family embarked on a voyage to Portugal. He died in Lisbon on October 8, 1754. During the tour, however, he kept a journal, *A Journal of a Voyage to Lisbon,* which is his last bequest to a world that sadly needs spirits as gallant as was Henry Fielding's.

He was an aristocrat—with an awareness of all that was wrong with the stratified society of his day. He was a man with serious convictions—who understood the importance of a sense of humor. He was a religious man—who wondered about the spiritual and intellectual chaos created by professional men of religion.

He is a man of permanent importance to our world.

TOM JONES: A SUMMARY

BOOK I

THE BIRTH OF THE HERO AND AN ACCOUNT OF THE ALLWORTHY FAMILY

Five years before the story opens, Mr. Allworthy, owner of one of the largest estates in Somersetshire and a man noted for his benevolence and piety, had lost his beloved wife. She had borne him three children, but all had died in infancy, so the Squire had the companionship of his sister, Bridget, who is more than a little ostentatious in her religious professions. "She was of that species of women whom you commend rather for good qualities than beauty. . . . Indeed, she was so far from regretting want of beauty that she never mentioned that perfection, if it can be called one, without contempt; and would often thank God she was not as handsome as Miss Such-a-one, whom perhaps beauty had led into errors, which she might have otherwise avoided."

Business obligations called Squire Allworthy to London and detained him there for "a full quarter of a year." Returning to the country, he was astonished as he prepared to retire for the night to discover an infant in his bed. He promptly summoned one of his servants, Mrs. Deborah Wilkins, to attend to the child's needs. Venomous, vindictive, and sanctimonious, Mrs. Wilkins hopes for the discovery of the foundling's mother—and for her punishment. Her malevolence is vividly contrasted with Allworthy's mildness and charity.

On the morning after the strange discovery, the Squire told his sister about it, and announced his resolution to take care of the child and rear it as his own. Considering the rigidity of her "virtue" and her "severity of character," it is surprising that she approves her brother's plans.

Always two-faced and opportunistic, Mrs. Wilkins changes her tune. Whereas she had at first called the child a misbegotten wretch, now she finds it a "dear, sweet, pretty creature." She retains, however, her determination to ferret out the baby's mother. Her relentless inquiries at last direct her suspicions to a young lady in the neighborhood named Jenny Jones.

Jenny, not an especially comely girl, had an uncommonly fine mind. She had been for some years a servant in the household of a schoolmaster and had acquired a remarkable education for one of her station in life. Human nature being what it is, her learning and her accomplishments bred resentment in the village and made her an obvious target of conjecture.

Mrs. Wilkins' "case" against Jenny was strengthened by the fact that she had often been at Allworthy's house and had very recently "officiated as nurse to Miss Bridget, in a violent fit of illness."

It was not an especially strong case and was unlikely to satisfy the scrupulously just Allworthy. It was strong enough for the meddlesome Wilkins, however, who, having summoned Jenny, began, before giving her a hearing, "You audacious strumpet." Curiously, instead of defending herself, Jenny freely confessed "the whole fact with which she was charged."

Brought before Allworthy in his capacity as local magistrate, Jenny, instead of being sent to prison as her detractors hoped she would be, was treated with the utmost leniency.

The Squire felt that he satisfied his duties by giving the hapless girl wholesome admonitions and spiritual advice. Eavesdropping on the interview were Mrs. Wilkins and Miss Bridget. Not surprisingly, Mrs. Wilkins was outraged by what she considered her master's condoning of vice; surprisingly, Bridget, who was usually no less stern than Mrs. Wilkins, was gratified by her brother's conduct.

Not only did Allworthy refrain from punishing Jenny but also he made it possible for her to remove herself from the neighborhood and start life afresh. First, however, he inquired into the paternity of the foundling but Jenny would only tell him that the man "was entirely out of his reach."

COMMENT: This brings a clearly unified section of the first book to a close. The locale has been established, ethical questions have been raised, the reader's curiosity has been aroused. The pace of the story is rapid, but the author frequently interrupts his narrative to comment on the relevance of various events to our understanding of human nature.

Tom Jones is divided into eighteen "Books," following the example of the classical epic. The first chapter of each book assumes the form of a monologue addressed by the author to the reader. In these first chapters Fielding talks about a variety of subjects in a relaxed, offhand manner that masks deeply held convictions about life and art. In the first chapter of Book I, for example, he amusingly represents himself as one "who keeps a public ordinary" (what we would call a restaurant), and the chapter is his "bill of fare." There is, he says, only one "article" offered—human nature. But dishes can be prepared in an indefinite number of ways and the prospective diner, therefore, need not have apprehensions over a lack of variety.

In connection with this, Fielding explicitly announces that he intends to exhibit human behavior as it is found in the country and also as it is found in cities. Since great cooks first set plain things before their hungry guests and then proceed to "the very quintessence of sauce and spices," this book opens with an account of country manners and hence the setting of the story in Somersetshire, one of the western counties of England with which Fielding was thoroughly familiar.

Allworthy is obviously an idealized character. He represents the kind of practical religion that Fielding considered the only kind of religion worth serious attention. Bridget Allworthy makes a great display of religion but she is narrow-minded, self-satisfied, and essentially uncharitable. Deborah Wilkins is even worse. She is obsequious and savage. She looks upon sin as a personal affront and she exults in the punishment of sinners.

Jenny Jones, the self-confessed mother of the infant found in Allworthy's bed, remains enigmatic. The reader is compelled to wonder why the mystery (or at least part of the mystery) of the hero's birth is revealed so early in the story. And why are we told of her education? What is the relevance of this information to the story? (Since Fielding is obviously a craftsman, every detail in the narrative must have relevance.)

Two devices used by Fielding, not only in this section of the book but also throughout, call for special comment. One is irony. Jenny, for example, is suspected of being a bad girl only because she is educated. Related to the insistent ironic tone that runs through the book is the author's use of a style that is called "mock-heroic." It is the inflated, grand style of the serious epic applied to ludicrous, non-heroic actions or situations. An example is to be found in Chapter VI, which describes Mrs. Wilkins' determined search for the mother of the foundling:

> "She with stately steps proudly advances over the field: aloft she bears her towering head . . ."

One final comment on this section. Fielding persuades his readers that he is completely candid. He seems to strike the pose of the omniscient author, that is, he pretends to know everything about his characters, their innermost thoughts and their total histories. But for the purposes of his story, to build up suspense and to prepare for surprises and sudden discoveries, he does not tell all that he knows until he wants to. Why, for example, are we told that Jenny Jones *had* worked as a servant for a schoolmaster? Why was Bridget so surprisingly willing to go along with her brother's plan to adopt the foundling? Could there be some special meaning to Jenny's telling Allworthy that the infant's father was "entirely out of his reach"? Properly to enjoy this novel, the reader ought always to be alert not only to what the author tells him but also to what the author does not tell him.

BOOK I

THE CONTINUATION OF THE ACCOUNT OF THE ALLWORTHY HOUSEHOLD

In the tenth chapter of the first book we are introduced to a peculiarly odious character who has taken advantage of Allworthy's charity: Dr. Blifil, a thoroughgoing charlatan and parasite, trained in medicine but disinclined to practice it since it was so much easier to accept the Squire's hospitality by posing as a great scholar with special interests in religion. Dr. Blifil became a kind of permanent guest in the Allworthy house and his pretentious discourses on theological manners endeared him to Miss Bridget. Acutely aware of the fact that Bridget was likely to inherit her brother's extensive fortune, Dr. Blifil ardently wished to marry her. Unhappily, there were two obstacles: he had, some ten years earlier than this story, married a woman who was still alive—and Allworthy knew about this marriage.

Frustrated, he recollected that he had a younger brother who had been a Captain in the Army but had sold his commission and "had betaken himself to studying the Scriptures, and was not a little suspected of an inclination to Methodism." Dr. Blifil managed to introduce the Captain into the Allworthy household. Everything went according to plan. In less than a month the Captain and Bridget were man and wife. Subsequent developments, however, were anything but according to Dr. Blifil's plan. The Captain had no intension of sharing the fortune now, as he thought, within his grasp with his brother. Taking full advantage of his privileged position in the household, he daily made life more and more intolerable for his brother. Dr. Blifil finally gave up, left the Allworthys, went up to London, and shortly thereafter died of a broken heart.

COMMENT: With the Blifils, Fielding continues his biting attack on varieties of religious hypocrisy, with at least a veiled reference to the Methodists, who were, at the time, the subject of much controversy. He also enriches his comedy of manners by subtly calling attention to the haste with which Bridget Allworthy, upwards of thirty years, accepted Captain Blifil's proposal of marriage, and by his exposure of some of the motives of marriage, notoriously avarice.

Dr. Blifil's "sad" end represents a convenient way of getting him out of the story after he had played his part and the author had no further use for him. It is also a kind of parody on "poetic justice" (the kind of completely logical and tidy justice one is more likely to encounter in books than in life). It is also a kind of parody on the sentimental tradition. There is something supremely ridiculous in the scheming, greedy, sycophantic Dr. Blifil's dying "of a broken heart."

BOOK II

THE FIRST TWO YEYARS AFTER THE MARRIAGE OF BRIDGET

In the first chapter, Fielding calls his book a "history," largely to allow himself some sardonic remarks about the wearisome prolixity of many historians, to direct gibes at modern journalism, and to camouflage the actual structural complexity of his narrative.

Eight months after her clandestine marriage to Captain Blifil, Bridget bears him a son. Squire Allworthy proposes that his nephew be brought up with the foundling whom he has, in his benevolence, adopted and given his own Christian name, Thomas. The proposal is agreeable to Bridget but rankles the fortune-hunting Blifil.

Meanwhile, Deborah Wilkins is relentlessly trying to find out who is Tom's father. Her suspicions finally settle upon the schoolmaster in whose house Jenny Jones had worked and who had helped her acquire an unusually good education. The schoolmaster, a Mr. Partridge, was a good-natured man, but had much to contend with. He was desperately poor and he had a jealous and shrewish wife.

Mrs. Partridge bitterly resented the attentions her husband was showing Jenny, accused him of misconduct with her, and discharged the innocent girl. Although his wife's suspicions were totally without foundation, Partridge was not altogether displeased with her action, for Jenny was becoming a far better scholar than he was himself.

After the departure of Jenny, peace reigned for a time in the Partridge home, but one day, while out shopping, Mrs. Partridge heard gossip to the effect that Jenny Jones had borne two bastards—not one but two! And this only nine months since she had been discharged!

Mrs. Partridge races home and beats poor Partridge unmercifully. In the wild battle she becomes covered with blood from her husband's wounds and bursts out of her stays. Neighbors rush in, and Partridge is thought, especially by the women, to be a vicious wife-beater.

Rumors spread rapidly and truth suffers as stories multiply. Mrs. Wilkins had heard about the Partridge affair, but Mrs. Partridge had once been a servant in the Allworthy home and had somehow offended Mrs. Wilkins who was, accordingly, reluctant to speak favorably of her old enemy. But realizing that Captain Blifil was in a fair way to being the heir of the wealthy Allworthy and wishing to ingratiate herself with him, she finally disclosed to him the story that Partridge was the father of the bastard who was being so indulged by Allworthy and who might well come into some of the estate Captain Blifil had set his heart upon. The Captain thought that it might be more strategic to have the Squire hear the story from someone else, but when Allworthy did not learn of the suspicions that had fastened on Partridge, Blifil finally told him.

Partridge is brought to trial before Allworthy, the magistrate. His wife testifies that he has confessed his guilt to her. Partridge protests that he confessed only because his wife had badgered him to the point where he could endure the horrors of his domestic situation no more and was prepared to confess to anything if such a confession would bring him a little peace and quiet. He insists that Jenny Jones will testify to his innocence, but by this time Jenny has left the neighborhood and nobody knows where she has gone.

The evidence against Partridge seems overwhelming to Allworthy. The Squire feels obliged to find the schoolmaster guilty and to dismiss him from his post. Shortly thereafter, Partridge's wife dies of the smallpox, and Partridge, freed from his responsibilities as husband, leaves the village to seek his fortune elsewhere.

The honeymoon over, Captain and Mrs. Blifil come to hate one another. The Captain has only one interest in life: getting his hands on Allworthy's fortune. He daydreams about all the things that he will do when he comes into his inheritance. But, ironically, he suddenly drops dead of apoplexy.

> **COMMENT:** The second book further develops the plot by introducing a second infant, young Blifil, foreshadowing the rivalry between Blifil and Tom, and by focusing attention on the unfortunate schoolmaster, Partridge, unjustly accused of being Tom's father. The scenes between Patridge and his wife allow Fielding an opportunity to display his talent for knockabout farce.

BOOK III

". . . THE MOST MEMORABLE TRANSACTIONS . . . FROM THE TIME WHEN TOMMY JONES ARRIVED AT THE AGE OF FOURTEEN, TILL HE ATTAINED THE AGE OF NINETEEN . . ."

As Tom Jones grew up, he exhibited a certain talent for getting into trouble. The decorous members of Allworthy's household were of the opinion "that he was certainly born to be hanged." The opinion was "justified" by the fact that he had already committed three *terrible* robberies—of an orchard, of a duck, and of a ball from Master Blifil!

Young Blifil, on the other hand, was "a lad of a remarkable disposition; sober, discreet, and pious beyond his age."

In his recklessness, zest for life, and love of sport, Tom, while shooting partridge one day, inadvertently trespasses and thus commits the crime of poaching. Game laws in the eighteenth century were very strict and Allworthy took the laws very seriously. Tom's guilt was beyond question. But Tom had been accompanied by Allworthy's own gamekeeper, and, prompted by his notions of honor, Tom refused to divulge the identity of his confederate. For his obstinacy he was severely beaten by his tutor, the Reverend Mr. Thwackum, whose whipping "fell little short of the torture with which confessions are in some countries extorted from criminals."

Thwackum's stern views on religion and duty were not the only views expressed in the Allworthy household. Another recipient of Allworthy's largesse was the philosophical Mr. Square, who held "human nature to be the perfection of all virtue," and maintained that "vice was a deviation from our nature."

The boyhood rivalry of Blifil and Tom is next explored. Though younger, Blifil is larger than Tom, but Tom is, physically, the more adroit. Tom, nevertheless, avoids quarrels with Master Blifil. He was "an inoffensive lad amidst all his roguery" and he "really loved Blifil." But one day, in "a difference arising at play between the two lads," Blifil called Tom a "beggarly bastard," and Tom, who "was somewhat passionate in his disposition," promptly bloodied Blifil's nose.

Vindictively, Blifil, in his complaint against Tom, told his uncle and Thwackum something that had been told him in confidence: that

Tom's confederate in the poaching incident was Black George, Allworthy's gamekeeper.

Black George is discharged. Tom's support of George, however, is applauded in the neighborhood, and the underhandedness of Blifil is universally condemned. As time goes on, it becomes increasingly clear that Bridget, Blifil's mother, detests her son but is very partial to Tom.

Time goes on. Tom does what he can to support the unfortunate gamekeeper and his family. The generous Allworthy, when he learns of the utter destitution of George, is on the point of re-engaging him, when Blifil reports that George has been poaching on Squire Western's estate —the same estate that Tom had trespassed upon.
In spite of Tom's offense, Western, lusty, gusty sportsman that he was, had kind feelings toward Tom. Accordingly, Tom had no hesitation about approaching Western to plead for his friend, Black George.

COMMENT: In this third book Fielding makes explicit some of his controlling ideas. For example, in discussing Thwackum and Square, he says: "Upon the whole, it is not religion or virtue, but the want of them, which is here exposed. Had not Thwackum too much neglected virtue, and Square, religion, in the composition of their several systems; and had not both utterly discarded all natural goodness of heart, they had never been represented as the objects of derision in this history . . ."

Tom Jones is about "natural goodness of heart." Tom has human frailties. He errs. Like all of us, given the inquisitorial spirit that still prevails, he was "born to be hanged." He steals apples. He is carried away by his enthusiasm for sport and poaches. But he has a code of honor.

Blifil is, on the other hand, "good." But what is his code? What do we mean by "good"? And what of the debates between Thwackum and Square?

Thwackum's meditations, we are told, "were full of birch." Is this how morals should be taught? Should we beat children into goodness? Square believed in "the natural beauty of virtue." Does this mean anything at all? Fielding questions the value of the muscular Christianity of his time; he also questions the value of Shaftesbury's belief that virtue is largely a question of good manners. (Anthony Ashley Cooper, Third Earl of Shaftesbury [1671-1713], was one of the most influential Deists of the eighteenth century and urged moral opinions of a notably optimistic and sentimental nature.)

BOOK IV

THE EVENTS OF THE FOLLOWING YEAR

Squire Western had an only daughter, Sophia, a beautiful and charming girl of eighteen whose upbringing had been supervised by Western's sister, a lady "thoroughly acquainted with the world, having lived in her youth about the court, whence she had retired some years since into the country." Tom, Blifil, and Sophia had long been acquainted with one another, in fact had grown up as playfellows. "The gaiety of Tom's temper suited better with Sophia than the grave and sober disposition of Master Blifil." Once some years before, Tom had given Sophia a little bird he had tamed and taught to sing. She became inordinately fond of the bird, and Blifil, resenting her preference for Tom over himself, one day maliciously released it from its captivity. Tom immediately climbed a tree on which the bird had perched; a branch broke and Tom fell into the canal beneath. Sophia's screams attracted the attention of Allworthy and Thwackum, who were dining at Squire Western's, and Thwackum immediately began beating poor Tom who "stood drooping and shivering before him." Allworthy interposed and asked young Blifil what had happened. Blifil sanctimoniously explained that he had released the bird because it was cruel and unchristian to keep it in captivity, and deceitfully added that he had not known Sophia was so fond of it. He also told the company that when Tom fell the bird had flown away and had been destroyed by a nasty hawk. Western was furious at Blifil.

COMMENT: In the first chapter of this book Fielding, in mock-serious fashion, discourses on the advantages of stylistic variety in a long narrative: it keeps the reader awake. He proceeds to invent a comical label for his "new" species of writing: this novel is none other than an "heroic, historical, prosaic poem." Although it is obvious that Fielding is joking, it is also obvious that he is seriously alerting the reader to the structural and stylistic complexity of the book and is relating it to the epic tradition.

With respect to variety, for example, it will be noted that the story of Sophia's pet bird is told in a flashback. The story also underlines the generosity and courage of Tom and the detestable hypocrisy of Blifil.

The incident of the bird also precipitates a pedantic debate between Thwackum and Square which is bitingly satirical on the narrow-mindedness of the participants.

The story resumes. At the end of the third book we learned of Tom's hope of getting Black George a position as Squire Western's gamekeeper. Instead of going directly to Western, Tom approached Sophia and solicited her help, which she gladly promised.

For all his boorishness, Western dearly loved his daughter and was particularly fond of having her play on the harpsichord for him. She always dutifully responded to his requests, though she had little relish for the uncouth tunes he favored.

The evening of Tom's visit, she "played all his favourites three times over," and was without any difficulty able to fulfill her promise to Tom. Fielding at this stage of the story has made it abundantly clear that Sophia is in love with Tom. He, however, while not insensible of her charms, can scarcely be said to be in love with her. Indeed, "his heart was in the possession of another woman, Molly Seagrim, a daughter of Black George, esteemed "one of the handsomest girls in the whole country."

Molly was not only a handsome girl; she was a remarkably forward girl. Tom was a passionate young man but he also had a nice sense of honor and did not want to take advantage of young innocence. But he could not hold out against her wiles and importunities and soon, without ever quite knowing how it all happened, was involved in an affair with the wanton Molly. "This, then, was the true reason of that insensibility which he had shown to the charms of Sophia . . . for, as he could not think of abandoning his Molly, poor and destitute as she was, so no more could he entertain a notion of betraying such a creature as Sophia."

It was soon apparent that Molly was pregnant. When Tom visited Sophia to plead the cause of Black George, Sophia, moved by the plight of the Seagrim family, had sent them some clothing. Now Molly's mother, hoping to conceal her daughter's condition, clothes her in one of Sophia's dresses. Molly, shameless hussy, was delighted and flaunted her elegance before her fellow villagers at Sunday church.

Western and his daughter were present, and Sophia was much struck by Molly's beauty, not observing that she was pregnant, and, sorry that the girl was the object of local spite and malice, offered to engage her as a servant. Black George, who was aware of his daughter's condition, was at a loss to know what to say to the offer.

Meanwhile, after Allworthy had left the village church, the local women gathered and marched against Molly. A battle royal occurred, described with great relish in mock-heroic style by Fielding. Square, Blifil, and Tom happen by, and Tom rushes to the rescue of Molly, who, by this time, is half-naked. He wraps her in his coat and dispatches a servant for a side-saddle so that he might carry her home. Blifil is annoyed that Tom should send the servant on an errand, for he is the only attendant that the three men had with them. Square, however, seconded Tom's order.

Sophia's offer of a position in her household to Molly brings on another battle in the Seagrim home, but Molly adamantly refuses to go into service.

On the following day, Tom, as he often did, hunted with Squire Western and accepted the Squire's invitation to dinner. Also present at dinner was Parson Supple, the curate of Allworthy's parish, "a good-natured, worthy man, but chiefly remarkable for his great taciturnity at table, though his mouth was never shut at it." When he had satisfied his mammoth appetite, Supple told the story of the churchyard fray and reported that Molly was "at the eve of bringing forth a bastard." Tom gets up and leaves unceremoniously, and Western at once guesses that he is the father of the unborn child. Sophia, having observed "Tom's colour change at the parson's story," was certain that the guess was accurate and begged her father's permission to be excused from attendance upon him for the rest of the day. This was granted, but reluctantly, for Western "scarce ever permitted her to be out of his sight, unless when he was engaged with his horses, dogs, or bottle."

On his return to his own home, Tom meets a constable who is carrying out the orders of Magistrate Allworthy that Molly be committed to a House of Correction. Tom brings her back to the Squire and begs for his compassion, confessing himself the father of the child she is bearing. Moved by "the honour and honesty of his self-accusation," Allworthy accedes to the request, but he did not fail to "read Tom a very severe lecture on this occasion."

> **COMMENT:** The Molly Seagrim affair proves to be only the first of such affairs that Tom finds himself entangled in before the story comes to its happy ending. Fielding is obviously not interested in condoning his hero's weaknesses. He is interested in establishing the fact that his hero is a man of flesh and blood, a man with normal instincts. Fielding makes it clear, too, that Molly, not Tom, was the aggressor. A saintly hero would resist temptation, but Tom is not a saint.
>
> On the other hand, he is not a depraved sinner. There are, in Fielding's view, worse sins than sins of the flesh. And Tom has attractive compensating virtues. He is compassionate. He is always capable of the graceful gesture. He is instinctively kind. He is totally honest.

The sketch of Squire Western as a rough, uncouth, foul-mouthed, hard-drinking, insensitive country squire is superb. But even Western has his virtues: he genuinely loves his daughter, and he is responsive to the merits of Tom. He recognizes the cowardly self-centeredness of Blifil and the manliness of Tom. He likes to hunt (i.e., to ride to the hounds) with Tom.

Sophia, not unnaturally, finds her father's amusement at the discovery that Tom is the father of Molly's bastard peculiarly offensive and painful. But Sophia will prove to be something much more than a symbol of feminine delicacy. She proves capable of moral action, important moral action. She proves able to forgive, to come to terms with the fact of imperfection in human beings.

In this section, as in many other parts of the novel, Fielding introduces information the meaning of which eludes the reader. For example, why does Square surprisingly take the side of Tom against Blifil when Tom sends the servant for a side-saddle?

While keeping to her room, Sophia is tormented by her maid, Mrs. Honour, who insists upon telling her all of the details of the scandal the whole village is talking about. Sophia professes herself utterly uninterested in the activities of Tom Jones but is obviously having a very difficult time removing him from her thoughts.

Western was so immoderately fond of his daughter that he persuaded her to join himself and Tom in their hunting expeditions. Although she thought the sport "too rough and masculine," and although she was reluctant to be in company with Tom, she consented. One day, however, her horse became too mettlesome and she was in danger of being thrown to the ground. Noticing her situation, Tom galloped to her assistance, jumped from his horse, and caught her before she fell.

His brave action, however, cost him a broken arm. Sophia was forced not only to be grateful to Tom for her own safety but also to be sorry for him because of the injury he had sustained.

Tom was brought back to Squire Western's home. A surgeon is summoned and it is determined that Tom had best stay with the Westerns until his arm is healed.

In one of her garrulous conversations with her mistress, the maid, Mrs. Honour, reveals that Tom was observed by her kissing one of Sophia's muffs, thus giving proof of his love of Sophia.

COMMENT: Notable among the numerous characters who people *Tom Jones* are the servants. The malevolence of Deborah Wilkins has already been mentioned. Sophia's maid is impertinent, untrustworthy, and stupid. Fielding was well aware of the fact that in his century the so-called upper classes were often callous and cruel toward the laboring classes, but his vision of life was fundamentally anti-sentimental and on the one hand he refuses to make his hero a saint while on the other hand he refuses to say that servants are paragons of virtue. He is concerned with affirming that representatives of all classes are frail human beings, mixtures of vices and virtues.

BOOK V

THE NEXT HALF YEAR

Tom has many visitors during his convalescence. Squire Allworthy called almost every day and used his time well. He lectured Tom, "in the mildest and tenderest manner," on his many deviations from a strict code of virtue. Thwackum was also "pretty assiduous in his visits," and he too seized the opportunity to lecture Tom. "His style, however, was more severe than Mr. Allworthy's." And Square, predictably, found the recumbent and defenseless Tom an admirable audience for his philosophical disquisitions on such subjects as the unworthiness of a broken bone the serious consideration of a wise man. Blifil occasionally visited Tom, but never came alone. He "cautiously avoided any intimacy, lest . . . it might contaminate the sobriety of his own character." Hearty Squire Western, when he could spare the time from hunting, called upon his guest, usually to offer him a mug of beer, which he considered an infallible medicine for "youth, health, and beauty." After a sleepless night, he resolves "to all ailments.

His most welcome visitor was Sophia, who played to him on her harpsichord. It becomes increasingly clear to Tom that he is really in love with Sophia and that she returns his love.

The course of true love, as the saying goes, never runs smoothly. Tom is aware of the fact that Sophia is heiress to a very great fortune, and that her hard-headed father has no intention of letting her marry a foundling with few if any prospects. He also remembers his responsibilities to Molly Seagrim—and he is not unmindful of Molly's abide by Molly, and to think no more of Sophia."

The following day, Mrs. Honour visits Tom and tells him of Sophia's fondness of the muff which Tom had sentimentally kissed. That very evening, while Sophia is playing on the harpsichord for her father and Tom is of the company, the favorite muff, which she is wearing on her arm, slips and interferes with the music. Western, annoyed by the interference with one of his favorite songs, picks up the muff and throws it into the fire. Sophia, however, quickly rescues it from the flames. The action forces Tom to have second thoughts about his decision concerning Molly and Sophia.

As an honorable young man, however, he realizes that he has obligations to Molly. He decides that a gift of money might be welcome to her in view of the family's desperate poverty. So when his arm was sufficiently recovered, he slipped away from Western's house one day and visited the Seagrims. Molly's sister, with a somewhat casual attitude toward propriety, directed Tom to Molly's room where she was, reportedly, "a-bed." Tom, having no special objection "to this situation of his mistress," went up to her room. He greeted her affectionately, and tried to explain why their affair had to be terminated, but Molly became wrathful. Somehow or other, while she was upbraiding Tom, she dislodged the curtain of her little closet, and there, hunched over in the most ludicrous of positions, was the philosophical Mr. Square. Molly's promiscuity has solved Tom's problems for the time being, and, though he is amused at Square's embarrassment, he promises not to betray his secret.

Tom later discovers that he was far from being the first to enjoy the favors of Molly and that it is far from certain that he is the father of her bastard. Relieved, he feels that he can tell Sophia that he loves her.

> **COMMENT:** Fielding's attitude toward Allworthy is difficult to define. He describes him as a thoroughly good, kind, benevolent man, but there are times when his goodness becomes a little oppressive, as when he lectures Tom on his misdeeds while Tom is trying to regain his health. Allworthy's timing sometimes seems less than perfect.
>
> The discovery of Square's turpitude represents Fielding's caustic comment on the vast difference between philosophical theories of virtue and the actual practise of virtue. The discovery of Molly's sluttishness represents an important stage in Tom's growing up. He is forced to look at things as they are, not as he would like to think that they are. Regrettably or not, rose-colored glasses have to be discarded.

The next important development in the story is the serious illness of Squire Allworthy. The family is summoned to what may be his deathbed and the Squire tells them what is in his will. Of all the immediate family, only Allworthy's sister Bridget is absent.

The bulk of Allworthy's extensive estate is to go to his nephew, young Blifil; Tom Jones is to receive £1,000 outright and to have an annual income of £500, a not inconsiderable sum in an age when some parsons had livings worth little more than £50 a year. Square, Thwackum, and the servants were included in the will.

Allworthy's generosity is, ironically, not appreciated. Mrs. Wilkins, Thwackum, and Square are all dissatisfied. In the midst of the rancorous discussion of the terms of the will, Blifil, who has left the sickroom, returns with the news that he has just been informed by a lawyer, named Mr. Dowling, that his mother has died.

Warned by the doctor that he should not upset his uncle, Blifil insists on giving Allworthy an account of Bridget's death. Tom is enraged at what he considers the thoughtlessness and imprudence of Blifil, but is relieved when there are signs that Allworthy's condition is improving. He is so happy at the turn of the events that he drinks too much at dinner and gets into a fight with Blifil.

Still drunk, but anxious to behave moderately, Tom goes out for a walk. It is a lovely June night, and Tom, reflecting on the obstacles that keep him, and will probably always keep him, from Sophia, bewails his unhappy fate. While he lies on the ground, brooding, Molly Seagrim suddenly comes upon him. Unsettled as he is by drink and by his despair, he is lured by Molly into a nearby grove.

Unhappily, Blifil and Thwackum had also decided on a walk in the pleasant summer evening. Blifil sees Tom and Molly (though he does not recognize her he is at least positive as to her sex) disappearing into the bushes.

Thwackum and Blifil follow Tom. Protecting his fellow-sinner, Tom strikes Blifil, and a furious battle ensues, with the numerical odds against Tom. Squire Western, Sophia, her aunt, and Parson Supple happen to be passing by. Inquiring into the cause of the quarrel, Western discovers Molly. Sophia "found herself very faint." Tom, nonetheless, cheerfully accepted Western's invitation "to go and sup with him."

> **COMMENT:** The section just described contrasts Tom's sincere love of Allworthy with the odious selfishness of the other members of the household. But again, Fielding refuses to represent his hero as more than human. He is so jubilant at the news of his godfather's recovery that he throws prudence to the winds, drinks to excess, gets into an unseemly fight with Blifil, and then tries to "cool off." Ironically, while meditating on the beauties and

charms of his beloved—but absent—Sophia, he is approached by the accommodating Molly.

What interests Fielding is this parodox. On the one hand, Tom is genuinely in love with Sophia and is thoroughly aware of her merits. On the other hand, Molly is available. An attractive girl, she is anything but a romantic figure. We are explicitly told that she appeared "in a shift that was somewhat of the coarsest, and none of the cleanest. . ."

The reader should keep in mind that Fielding is, among other things, exposing the essential falseness of the romantic and sentimental view of life. *Tom Jones* is much more than a rebuttal of Richardson's novels; but surely a revulsion from the saccharine quality of much of Richardson's work accounts for incidents in Fielding's finest novel.

BOOK VI

CONTAINING ABOUT THREE WEEKS

Up to this book, the events in this novel have been confined to Somersetshire, to the vast estates of Western and Allworthy, and to their villages. Fielding has faithfully described eighteenth-century English country life, in all its rawness and coarseness, but not with excessive emphasis on earthiness. There is always the lovely Sophia. Tom possesses natural grace. Allworthy is not only a good man, a judicious magistrate, but also a supporter of learning. And Thwackum and Square, though in general caricatures, remind us that there were *some* ideas (whatever we may think of them) in the country. But now Fielding wishes to expand his narrative, to change his locale. In this book Tom begins his journey—his journey from youthful folly to prudence, his journey from the casual affairs that man's frailty can occasion, his journey in search of his identity.

The events of the book can be quickly summarized. Squire Western's officious and opinionated sister decides that Sophia is in love, as indeed she is. But inasmuch as Blifil is Allworthy's heir, it is obvious to Mrs. Western that Sophia is in love with Blifil. Squire Western likes Tom and dislikes Blifil, but even he can see the practical advantages of a match with Blifil. He falls in with his sister's plans.

Negotiations begin, but once Sophia sees what is afoot, she runs to her room and vehemently protests that she will never marry a man she hates. Western, frustrated in his great expectations, is furious, and, learning that Sophia loves Tom, turns against his young friend. Blifil, frustrated in his expectations, spitefully tells Allworthy about the misbehavior of Tom, i.e., his drunkenness, when Allworthy was, as he thought, on his deathbed. He also tells about Tom's encounter with Molly.

Allworthy feels that, in justice, he can no longer be merciful to Tom. He sternly dismisses him from his household, but gives him a piece of paper that is, in effect, a money order for £500.

Tom "accordingly set out, and walked above a mile, not regarding, and indeed scarce knowing, whither he went." He stopped by a little brook and "presently fell into the most violent agonies, tearing his hair from his head, and using most other actions which generally accompany fits of madness, rage, and despair."

In his paroxysm of grief he throws away the piece of paper which Allworthy had given him. Recovering somewhat, he decides that he must write a farewell note to Sophia, and goes to a nearby house where writing materials are made available to him. Searching his pockets for wax with which to seal the letter, he discovers that he has thrown his possessions away, and returns to the brook to search for them.

On his way to the brook he meets Black George, who "condoled with him on his misfortune" and helped him in his search, even though he knew that the valuable paper was in his own pocket, he having found it before meeting Tom.

Although George does not love Tom to the point of returning to him the £500 he had found, he agrees to deliver, through Mrs. Honour, the love-letter Tom had written to Sophia.

Western is so angry at his daughter's intransigence that he has locked her in her room. But Honour, her maid, of course, is allowed to be with her, and thus is able to give her Tom's letter and to tell her of Tom's penniless plight. Tender-hearted Sophia sends him, through Honour and George, sixteen guineas, all the money that she had, at the time, at her disposal.

George considered the advisability of keeping the sixteen guineas for himself but decided that he might be found out. He brings it to Tom.

> **COMMENT:** Fielding's indictment of humanity is simultaneously remorseless and good-natured. There is high comedy in Mrs. Western's interpretation of Sophia's symptoms, but there is also an appalling ugliness in her, and her brother's, naked greed. Blifil's malice was, of course, to be expected, but Black George's dishonesty is shocking when the reader reflects on how much Tom has done for him.

BOOK VII

CONTAINING THREE DAYS

Tom receives a letter from Blifil telling him that Squire Allworthy wishes him to leave the neighborhood. He decides to go to sea, hires horses, and sets out for Bristol.

Mrs. Western continues her efforts to promote the marriage of Blifil and Sophia. She cannot understand her niece's inability to perceive the practical advantages of the match. Squire Western himself is in no mood for mere argument. He demands that his daughter obey him.

Mrs. Western turns on her brother and berates him for his foolish interference in delicate matters that she feels she is much better able to understand. He in turn complains of her interference, and Mrs. Western in her anger prepares to leave the Western house.

The Squire complains to Sophia that he has always been unlucky in his relations with women. It turns out, however, as the narrator takes us back to Western's life with Sophia's mother, who had died when Sophia was eleven, that the Squire had been a brutal tyrant.

Sophia tries to reconcile her father and her aunt. When she suggests that Mrs. Western, who is a very wealthy woman and who has hitherto meant to leave her fortune to the Squire, is a passionate woman who may well feel disposed to change her will, the Squire rushes off to make at least a kind of peace with his sister.

Plans for the immediate marriage of Sophia to Blifil are made. With reference to Squire Allworthy's compliance it should be noted that he was totally ignorant of Sophia's detestation of Blifil.

Sophia plans to run away. Her maid, Mrs. Honour, is of two minds. Should she betray Sophia to her father—and reap the rewards she was certain would be forthcoming; or she should stay with Sophia—and hope for even greater rewards in the future?

Circumstances forced her decision. Honour got into a quarrel with Mrs. Western's personal maid, and Mrs. Western forced her brother to discharge Sophia's two-faced attendant. She packs and leaves the house, but agrees to meet Sophia "at a certain place not far from the house, exactly at the dreadful and ghostly hour of twelve."

In the meantime, Western and his sister are violent in their demands that Sophia get ready to marry Blifil. Western, indeed, was so violent that "he frightened her into an affected compliance with his will" which so pleased him that his frowns changed to smiles and he gave her a large sum of money "to dispose of in any trinkets she pleased."

> **COMMENT:** Sophia clearly represents Fielding's views on the nature of true love. Mrs. Western, for all of her self-conceit, is a foolish, short-sighted woman with essentially nasty views on marriage and with a totally erroneous conviction that all life is lived in terms of political connivance. Western is a boor and a brute. He loves his daughter but is incapable of recognizing her rights as a human being.
>
> Mrs. Honour is an obvious symbol of duplicity and can scarcely be said to engage our affections. But on the other hand, the arbitrariness with which Mrs. Western has her discharged reminds us of an obliviousness to social justice that prevailed in earlier centuries. Mrs. Western, for example, tells her brother that she once knew a justice of the peace in London who "would commit a servant to Bridewell at any time when a master or mistress desired it."

The rest of the book focuses attention on the first adventures of Tom Jones on the road. He has set out for Bristol, England's most important seaport, but loses his way and takes refuge in an inn.

There he meets a Quaker who tells him a sad story: his daughter has made a most imprudent marriage and he intends to disown her. Tom is amazed at the man's anger and malice and counsels him to show a more charitable disposition to his daughter and son-in-law. The Quaker is in turn amazed that Tom should be so lunatic as to think that a man should forgive a disobedient daughter foolish enough to marry a man of less property than the man her father wanted her to marry.

> **COMMENT:** The meeting with a Quaker is a very minor episode and seems somewhat unnecessarily to touch upon a theme already much exploited—that of religious hypocrisy. The Quaker, a member of the Society of Friends and a believer in peace, is, ironically, unable to live in peace with his own flesh and blood. The story that the Quaker tells Tom, of course, is especially poignant to him because of his own situation, and the daughter's defiance of her father parallels Sophia's defiance.
>
> It may be questioned, however, whether the incident really moves the story along or serves any satiric purpose that had not already been accomplished. Possibly Fielding for one reason or another had a special animus against Quakers.

While Tom is still at the inn, a band of soldiers enters and Tom decides to change his plans and join their ranks. He marches with them all the next day, and at night the soldiers repair to another inn where they join the officers who will command them. Tom, who has been brought up as a gentleman, behaves like a gentleman, is dressed like a gentleman, and cannot be treated like an ordinary volunteer. He is invited to dine with the officers.

During the the usual after-dinner t oasts, when all are more than a little warmed by wine, Tom proposes a toast to Sophia. One of the officers, in jest, claims that he knows Sophy Western, and, in the grossest terms, intimates that she is a woman of the most licentious character. Tom, naturally, protests, and the officer, Northerton by name, drunk and resentful of what he considers Tom's impertinence, throws a bottle at his head, knocking him unconscious.

A physician is summoned and Tom is bandaged and put to bed. Meanwhile, the commanding officer of the soldiers has ordered Northerton's arrest. He is confined to a room in the inn and an armed sentinel is stationed outside the door.

In the middle of the night, Tom, determined as a matter of honor to avenge himself on Northerton, slips out of his room and approaches Northerton's. The sentinel, believing the pale and blood-stained Tom to be a ghost, fires at him, luckily missing, and faints. The shot awakens everybody in the inn and in commotion it is discovered that Northerton has escaped and has absconded with the company's money.

The escape had been effected through the complicity of the landlady of the inn, who now, to cover up her own guilt, is vehement in her demand that the sentinel be punished. Tom, however, once more reveals the essential goodness of his heart by interceding for the sentinel. The soldiers again march off, leaving Tom to recuperate. He promises to join them as soon as he is able.

COMMENT: No reader has ever failed to notice the panoramic quality of *Tom Jones.* We have the country scenes: riding to the hounds, shooting, wenching, brawling; there are the gross pleasures of Squire Western, the smug complacency of his "politic" sister, the gracious paternalism of the good Squire Allworthy; there are servants, unlovely in their sanctimoniousness and selfishness and duplicity; there is the wordly and disgustlingly gluttonous Parson Supple; there is a paragon of unspoiled country girls, Sophia.

Then we have the eighteenth-century English road and the inns that provided at least a modicum of comfort for those who could or would confront the perils of that road. It is not surprising that Tom lost his way while traveling towards Bristol. Even experienced travelers in eighteenth-century England more often than not lost their way.

There is magnificent gusto in Fielding's accounts of inns. He is at his comic best in his depiction of landlords and landladies. He uses inns as the ideal setting for some of his most wildly rowdy scenes.

At this point in the story the reader should have become acutely conscious of Fielding's superb ear for the language of real life. He knows how coarse, uneducated country squires like Western talk. He knows the cant of unprincipled pretenders to learning like Thwackum and Square. He knows the affected speech of social upstarts like Mrs. Western. The dialogue in *Tom Jones* is one of the novel's chief delights.

A word should perhaps be said about the topical relevance of the soldiers. In 1688 the English people, in what came to be called the Glorious Revolution, turned against their monarch, James II. He had in many ways alienated their sympathies, and one (but only one) of his offenses was that he had become a Roman Catholic. James was driven into exile, but his descendants were slow to forget the legitimacy of their claim to the throne. The first serious effort to win back the crown by force was made in 1715. The second major (and still unsuccessful) "Jacobite" uprising took place in 1745. Fielding, writing immediately after the event, when the memory of the excitement and fears was still fresh, when the trials of some of the Scottish leaders of the Jacobite rebellion were still being conducted, has Tom begin his pilgrimage when all England was in a ferment because of the threat to law and order and the Established Church. It has already been suggested in these notes that Fielding may have had an animus against the Quakers, probably too an animus against Methodists; he also demonstrably had an animus against Catholics. This is not said to convict him of prejudice or religious bias. It is merely to report that Fielding shared, as one would expect him to share, the feelings of a good many of his contemporaries, and thus to make it easier for the twentieth-century reader to understand that Tom Jones' enthusiasm for enlisting in the army had a very special significance to Fielding's first readers.

BOOK VIII

CONTAINING ABOUT TWO DAYS

All of the introductory chapters to the individual books of *Tom Jones* are interesting and thought-provoking. The first chapter of this eighth book, however, is especially valuable for the student of Fielding's most deeply held convictions about the relationship of literature to life.

Although none of Fielding's joyously disenchanted remarks about human pettiness, avarice, and savagery should go unnoticed or unappreciated, it must be said that the most important feature of this eighth book is the re-introduction of Partridge the schoolmaster, hounded from his home and his position because it was believed that he was the father of Tom Jones.

Still recovering from his wounds, though not altogether welcome at the inn because, in spite of his gentlemanly appearance, he is, admittedly, almost penniless, Tom is attended by a barber known as Little Benjamin. The barber is an amusing fellow, with a propensity for quoting Latin, and Tom is quite taken with him.

From the landlady, the barber learns who Tom is. Subsequently, Tom gives Little Benjamin an account of his life, leaving out a few details such as his last encounter, in the grove, with the notorious Molly. The barber, in return, reveals that he is none other than Partridge the schoolmaster, and he assures Tom that the report that he was Tom's father was completely untrue. He proposes that he accompany Tom in his travels, being willing to act in the capacity of his servant even though Tom says that he has no money.

Fielding tells us that Partridge does not really believe the story that Tom had told him. Partridge was convinced that Tom was Allworthy's son and heir, and he hoped, by staying close to him, to ingratiate himself with the Squire and not only get back his former position as schoolmaster but also profit from Allworthy's widely heralded benevolence. Thus Tom's pilgrimage begins anew, now with Partridge as companion.

Once more, as night decends, the wayfarers avail themselves of the comforts on an inn. And here Tom meets two lawyers who recognize him; one of them is the Mr. Dowling who brought the news of Mrs. Blifil's death; the other is described by Fielding as a vile petty-fogger "without sense or knowledge of any kind." He had performed little pieces of business for Allworthy, but had never been entertained except in the kitchen. He gives the landlady of the inn a distorted and malicious account of Tom's history. Believing the story, she behaves so badly towards Tom that he determines to leave the inn forthwith, despite the objections of Partridge.

It is early evening in mid-winter and very cold. As night draws on, the travellers find themselves in an eerie part of the countryside. Spying a cottage, they hasten to it to solicit hospitality, and are admitted by an old woman.

Partridge, one of whose traits is that he is superstitious and credulous, is terrified; he is certain that they have entered the abode of a witch. The old woman, however, turns out to be only the housekeeper of an eccentric old man, a misanthrope who has completely cut himself off from the rest of humanity. She begs her visitors to leave, knowing how much her master detests all mankind. Before they can leave, however, they hear the Old Man's approach, hear that he is, as he nears his home, in grave trouble because he is set upon by thieves. Tom rushes out and saves the Old Man. Tom and Partridge are henceforth welcome guests. The Old Man explains how his own experiences of life, the greed and cruelty of men toward one another, had utterly soured him and made him what he had become.

> **COMMENT:** The meeting with the so-called Old Man of the Hill is an episode. It is, by design, not directly related to the plot, the main story-line, of *Tom Jones*. It is used, however, by Fielding for various purposes. It helps him to dramatize one of the important traits of Partridge—his superstition, his particular fear of ghosts. This, of course, helps Fielding to show that he is a man of an enlightened age. It also provides him with a weapon against the feared Catholics, who were, it was widely believed, exceedingly credulous.
>
> The story told by the Man of the Hill is also particularly interesting in that it echoes some of Fielding's own disillusionments in the fashionable world of London. He was, in a sense, incapable of becoming a misanthrope; he was also unable to subscribe to a romantic and rosy-eyed view of the world.
>
> Fielding also uses the encounter with the Man of the Hill in the development of his plot, as will soon become clear.

BOOK IX

CONTAINING TWELVE HOURS

The first chapter is another of the gems. Particularly important is Fielding's eighteenth-century convictions that a writer must have learned his trade, must be familiar with the literature of the past, must know his own world, must have a feeling for people.

He further explains why he calls his novel a "history" rather than a "romance." He feels that many romances are merely idle fictions, whereas he is interested in actually reporting the facts concerning Nature.

Tom Jones and the Man of the Hill go for an early morning walk. They hear the screams of a woman and Tom rushes to help her. A woman, stripped half naked, is struggling with a ruffffian who has put a garter around her neck and is attempting to draw her to a tree, presumably to hang her. With his trusty oaken stick Tom knocks the villain down and rains blows on him. He then observes that his antagonist is none other than Northerton, the army officer who had insulted Sophia and had thrown a bottle at Tom's head. Tom tied Northerton's hands behind his back with the garter he had been using to strangle his captive. Then he directs his attention to the woman, who reveals that she is "an entire stranger in that part of the world." Tom returns to the old man for advice and is told to escort the woman to the nearby town of Upton where he would be able to provide her "with all manner of conveniences." He agrees to do this and requests his host to direct Partridge to Upton and then goes back to the dishevelled woman. He discovers that in spite of the precautions he had taken, Northerton had managed to make his escape.

Tom offers the woman his coat, but she declines. Tom walks on ahead of her so as not to offend her modesty, but she needed his assistance over stiles and other obstacles so that he frequently had to turn around and could scarcely avoid being conscious of her somewhat considerable charms.

> **COMMENT:** Once again Fielding arouses the reader's curiosity. Who is this woman who was struggling with Northerton? What was Northerton's purpose in attacking her? Was she deliberately flaunting her semi-nakedness at Tom?
>
> As one reads further and further in *Tom Jones,* one is struck by Fielding's fondness for coincidence. This puts something of a strain on the reader's credulity but it should be observed that Fielding is not an altogether realistic writer. He combines realism with boisterous farce, with the use of caricatures, with wild improbabilities.

Arriving at an inn at Upton, Tom and his companion enter, but the landlady tries to drive them away. A battle royal ensues, with the landlady, the landlord, Susan the maid, Tom, and the bedraggled woman participating. Partridge comes in while the fight is going on, and he proceeds to get into it.

A coach carrying a young lady and her maid now arrives at the inn. They go immediately to the room assigned them, taking no notice of the assembled company; nor is Tom, busy trying to rescue Partridge from the fury of Susan, in a position to notice them.

At about this same time a group of soldiers, with a captured deserter, arrives at the inn and settle down in the kitchen, where Tom and the woman he had rescued were sitting, the woman now at least decently clad in a pillow-case. One of the soldiers recognizes her as "Captain Waters' lady." The landlady, overhearing the conversation between the soldier and Mrs. Waters and learning that in spite of her appearance she was an officer's wife and therefore a lady, hastened to make amends by offering her a gown.

In a very comic chapter Fielding next relates Mrs. Waters' seduction of Tom. Not having eaten for twenty-four hours, Tom at first is much more concerned with great masses of beef. When he has finished his heroic meal, however, he is more vulnerable to the wiles and blandishments of his amorous companion.

Meanwhile conversation is going on among the soldiers and Partridge in the kitchen of the inn. The sergeant in command of the unit reveals that there is some doubt about the legality of Mrs. Waters' marriage and that she had been having an affair with Northerton. Partridge, still laboring under a misconception, states that Tom is Allworthy's heir and is travelling incognito.

The young lady who had entered the inn just before the soldiers now feels suitably refreshed and orders her coach prepared for the resumption of her journey. The coachman, however, is drunk and completely unable to attend to his duties. The landlady, while waiting upon Tom and Mrs. Waters at tea, tells him of the girl's distress.

Fielding now interrupts his narrative to give us more information about Mrs. Waters. As the soldiers had intimated, there was some doubt as to whether she and the Captain really were man and wife. And she was involved in an affair with Northerton.

Captain Waters is the commanding officer of the company into which Tom Jones volunteered when he first fell in with the detachment of soldiers and had been introduced to Northerton. He is about to lead his company against the Jacobite rebels of 1745, and it is arranged that his wife will repair to Bath, a fashionable watering-place where there would be plenty of amusements, until his return.

Mrs. Waters agreed to accompany her "husband" as far as the city of Worcester. There she planned to have an assignation with Northerton when he and his men should march up to join the regiment. Northerton's misadventure with Jones upset the plans.

As soon as Notherton effected his escape he made off for Worcester and called on Mrs. Waters only a few hours after her husband had gone off to the wars. He, believing that he had killed Jones, told her of his mortal peril. She advised flight to the Continent and agreed to let him have some money, she having been well provided for to make possible her sojourn at Bath.

Northerton sets off in the general direction of Wales, where, in one of the seaports, he hopes to make arrangements to get passage to the Continent. He persuades Mrs. Waters to go at least part of the way with him. Utterly reckless and unscrupulous, he decides to kill his mistress for her money and valuables, including an expensive diamond ring;. and it was while he was trying to put this plan into effect that he had been encountered by Jones as he responded to the woman's screams.

COMMENT: That section of the narrative that has the inn at Upton as its setting is justly regarded as representative of Fielding's comic genius at its height. He is superb in creating scenes of riotous disorder, and the battle at Upton, described with the author's customary irony and in his mock-heroic manner, is one of his best.

The student of Fielding's art will do well to observe that if the novelist seems to be extremely circumstantial and leisurely in the depiction of certain incidents, at the same time he manages to achieve extraordinary rapidity and to crown his work with an almost bewildering number of characters and incidents.

Some readers have considered *Tom Jones* immoral because such things as the seduction of Tom by Mrs. Waters are described in a humorous way. There is no doubt that Fielding believed that there were many worse sins than those of the flesh. He detested hypocrisy, avarice, deceitfulness, meanness of spirit, and cowardice much more than he detested such things as a young man's yielding to the natural promptings of his human constitution.

It should further be emphasized that Fielding, though good-natured about Tom's failings, is not *seriously* condoning them. He exploits the failings for their comic value in relationship to the entire work and not in their relationship to an abstract ethical code. It is not, in other words, that sin in itself is comical, but Tom, in his naivete and guilelessness, being victimized by the profligate Molly Seagrim and thinking himself the wicked aggressor is funny. And Tom, deeply in love with the angelic Sophia but unable to resist the available charms and the wordly wiles of another wanton, Mrs. Waters, is funny.

The author's central point (or, at least, one of his central points) is that Tom Jones has good instincts, a naturally good heart. But he is young, inexperienced, and rather agreeably inflammatory. Who wants a cold hero? Blifil is among other things a device by which Fielding defines Tom.

To see Tom's wanderings from Allworthy's home to his final haven in the arms of his beloved Sophia as a symbolic pilgrimage is perhaps to be excessively serious about an essentially comic novel. But there is no question but what this work is a kind of secular Pilgrim's Progress. The point is that Fielding describes a progress. His pilgrim has to have a place to progress from, and that place is his inexperience and consequent injudiciousness.

The isolation of those incidents involving sex from the rest of this vast and sprawling novel ought to be challenged. The raucous sex in *Tom Jones* is part of Fielding's often grotesque portrait of a lusty, rambunctious age. Many writers of the eighteenth century stress the age's preoccupation with propriety, with politeness, with enlightened values. When we think of the century, however, we ought to realize that the number of philosophers was very limited. The number of elegant and refined artists and amateurs like Thomas Gray and Horace Walpole was limited. England was a predominantly agricultural country in the eighteenth century, and the age was an age of coarse farmers, greedy innkeepers, of highwaymen, of, in short, the kind of people we meet in *Tom Jones*.

Had Fielding left sex completely out of his novel he would have been culpably false to his intention of giving an honest picture of the world as he knew it. The perceptive reader will be much more aware of Fielding's relentless honesty and gratifying cheerfulness in a confessedly imperfect world than he will be of Tom's misadventures with women. He will also notice in this connection that there is nothing lubricous in Fielding's handling of sex. He is matter-of-fact.

BOOK X

ABOUT TWELVE HOURS MORE

In his customary mock-serious way, Fielding in the first chapter of this book warns against misunderstanding him. It will already have been noticed that there are many incidents in this novel. The premature critic may decide that the structure of the work, therefore, is too loose. In effect, he promises that by the end of the narrative everything will have been tied together in a tightly constructed plot.

Furthermore he anticipates criticism that he repeats himself. We meet various landlords and landladies, various servants, various soldiers. Fielding insists, however, that he not only includes "certain characteristics in which most individuals of every profession and occupation agree," but also marks the "nice distinctions" between them.

Finally, he reminds us that we ought not condemn a character "as a bad one because it is not perfectly a good one."

> **COMMENT:** It is clear that in his introductory chapters Fielding is partially amusing himself by teasing his readers. He is also giving his readers useful hints. For example, he is warning readers that almost every character who enters these pages has relevance to the plot and that therefore the story must be followed very closely. Thus in the ninth book just as the great battle of Upton is coming to an end, a lady and her maid descend from a coach and take shelter in the inn. Fielding explicitly tells us that they did not take notice of the combatants, nor were Tom and Partridge in a position to take notice of them. Readers may be tempted to suspect that the lady is Sophia, a suspicion that would give an added ironic touch to Tom's dalliance with Mrs. Waters. But are the visitors Sophia and Honour? We had best wait and see, but we had certainly best not forget this particular entrance.
>
> Fielding's answer to the imagined criticism that he repeats himself and introduces, for example, too many inns and comic landladies, is probably best interpreted as a complaint that too much of what passes for literary criticism is trivial and captious. The reader who wishes to do so, of course, if he has the leisure and the patience, may try to discover the "nice distinctions" the author promises. Considering the dimensions of the plot, however, and the significance of the main characters to what Fielding wishes to say about life, is to see that Fielding is merely being jocular in his promise but beneath the jocularity is striking back at foolish critics.
>
> His final injunction, that we see that characters in this world are mixtures of good and bad, is one of Fielding's serious convictions, a principle in his ethical teaching.

We are still in the inn at Upton. It is now midnight, and only Susan Chambermaid is still at her chores. All the other occupants of the inn are abed.

Suddenly a man enters and though wild and incoherent makes it known to Susan that he is pursuing a wife who has run away. Susan, jumping to the conclusion that Mrs. Waters is the errant wife, directs the aggrieved husband to her room. He bursts in, to discover Tom in the bed. At first he thinks that he has made a mistake, but then he notices articles of female clothing in the room and becomes more enraged than ever. He and Tom scuffle and Mrs. Waters screams.

In the room next to this one was an Irish gentleman who had stopped at the inn on his way to Bath, where he hoped to improve his fortune either at the gaming tables or by winning the hand of an heiress. Awakened by the uproar, he arms himself with a sword and enters the scene of the confusion. It quickly turns out that the Irishman, one Maclachlan, is acquainted with the outraged husband, greets him by name—Mr. Fritzpatrick, and calls his attention to the fact that the lady in the bed is not Fitzpatrick's wife.

Peace is not easily restored, however, for the landlady has also heard the uproar and enters the room and is forthwith engaged in a brawl with the affronted Mrs. Waters. Scrupulously anxious to defend the honor of his companion, Tom maintains that he had heard noises in Mrs. Waters' room and had just previously entered to protect her from apprehended harm. At length matters quiet down, the three gentlemen and the landlady retire, Tom to his room, Fitzpatrick and Maclachlan to Maclachlan's, and the landlady to get details of the story from Susan. Susan, who had led Fitzpatrick to Mrs. Waters' room, swears that she saw Tom jump out of Mrs. Waters' bed, whereupon she is soundly berated by the landlady who is now prepared to believe Partridge's story that Tom is Squire Allworthy's heir. And she is accordingly prepared to believe that Tom had heard noises and had gone to protect Mrs. Waters from thieves, for surely the other two "gentlemen" were thieves. If Fitzpatrick "had broke open the lady's door with any of the wicked designs of a gentleman, he would never have sneaked away to another room to save the expense of a supper and a bed to himself."

Fielding now tells us why Mrs. Fitzpatrick had run away from her husband. She had possessed a "very handsome" fortune, which Fitzpatrick had squandered except for a "pittance" she had managed to keep for herself and which he wished to get his hands on. He had treated her with such extreme cruelty that she at last felt oblige to escape.

It is ironical that Mrs. Fritzpatrick is at this moment in the inn. Her husband, having satisfied himself that the woman in Mrs. Waters' room was not his wife, presumed that she was not to be found in this public house.

Two more guests arrive, a beautiful young lady and her maid. The lady requests a room where she may refresh herself for a short time and then resume her journey. Both she and her maid are in riding clothes and are thus traveling on horseback rather than in a coach.

While the lady rests the maid goes to the kitchen for food. She behaves with the utmost insolence to everyone, including Partridge, who is there; and the landlady, resentful of this insolence, tells her that the inn is a very respectable inn, frequented by "people of great quality." For example, she goes on to tell the obnoxious maid that at this very moment the son and heir of Squire Allworthy is in the house.

The maid is skeptical, announcing that she knows Allworthy very well and knows that he does not have a son. Partridge, who has been giving out the story (the truth of which he believes), explains that the young man is, indeed, a bastard, but that Allworthy is his father and means to leave his estate to him, "as certainly as his name is Jones." On hearing the name, the maid is startled, hastily finishes her meal, and rejoins her mistress.

As the reader has doubtless guessed, the mistress is none other than Sophia, and the maid the treacherous Honour. When Sophia learns from her attendant that Tom Jones is in the house, she begs her to find a means of informing him that she would like to see him. Honour returns to the kitchen, but her behavior hitherto had been so offensive that everyone has come to the uncharitable conclusion that the most recent guests are a "couple of Bath trulls" and they sullenly refuse to obey her commands. She gets into a heated altercation with Partridge, who is goaded into telling her that Jones is in bed with a wench.

The vixenish Honour hurries back to Sophia to acquaint her with this news, and dwells upon the enormity of Tom's offenses, reminding her mistress of the affair with Molly Seagrim.

At first Sophia refuses to believe the story. Susan Chambermaid enters the room, however, and, being interrogated, confirms it. Once again Sophia's dignity and self-respect have been dealt a dreadful blow. Sophia keeps protesting that she is totally unconcerned over Jones' conduct, but she cries a great deal and is obviously deeply hurt.

She and Honour prepare to resume their travels, when suddenly she recollects that she has with her a muff, which she had once rescued from the fire and which Tom had been seen kissing (Book V). She hastily writes her name on a piece of paper, pins it to the muff, and bribes a servant to deposit it in Tom's empty bed (for he had indeed returned, after the tumults had subsided, to his "wench") to serve as a mute if eloquent accusation.

Early the next morning, while it is still dark, Tom slips back to his own room and summons Partridge to attend him. Partridge, a coward and a secret supporter of the Jacobite cause, tries to persuade Tom to abandon his intention of joining the army and to return home. Also, since he has become tired of walking, he proposes that they "borrow" a couple of horses from the stable of the inn.

Tom becomes angry at Partridge, who then tries to restore peace with bawdy jests. Last night, he tells Tom, a couple of wenches had proposed disturbing Tom's rest, but he had managed to prevent them. But, he goes on, they must have contrived to get into Tom's room in spite of him, for "here lies the muff of one of them." When Tom, who had not seen it before in the dark, recognized it, he nearly went out of his wits and furiously prepared to follow Sophia, ordering Partridge to hire horses "at any rate."

Meanwhile, Maclachlan and Fitzpatrick prepare to depart toward Bath. It is revealed that the coach which had carried the first lady and her maid to Upon had been rented by the lady and was now available for travelers to Bath. From his conversation with the coachman, Maclachlan comes to the conclusion that the coach had brought Fitzpatrick's wife to the inn. Being apprised of his friend's suspicion, Fitzpatrick once again races madly through the inn in frantic search for his wife, but she had already left at about the same time as Sophia. Once again this never-to-be-forgotten inn at Upton is the scene of a riotous chase as the wild Irishman fruitlessly pounds on door after door. And no sooner has he given up the chase when in comes a gentleman "hallooing as hunters do when the hounds are at a fault."

The gentleman just arrived "was no other person than Squire Western himself, who was come hither in pursuit of his daughter." Had he been two hours earlier he would have found not only Sophia but also his niece Harriet, for the unfortunate wife of Fitzpatrick was Western's niece and had, five years before, run away "out of the custody" of Mrs. Western.

Fitzpatrick and Western were unknown to one another. Both run madly about the house, one in search of his wife, the other in search of his daughter.

When both were in the kitchen, now "a scene of universal confusion," Jones entered with Sophia's muff in his hand. Western "set up the same holloa as is used by sportsmen when their game is in view." He laid hold of Tom and cried, "We have got the dog fox, I warrant the bitch is not far off."

Fitzpatrick, having learned who Western is and wishing to ingratiate himself with his uncle, says that Tom lies when he tells the Squire that he had not seen Sophia and did not know where she was. Fitzpatrick reports that he had come upon them in bed together and, to prove it, leads the company to Mrs. Waters' room. Mrs. Waters is convinced that she is in bedlam, screams again, but afterwards sensibly concludes that there is no possibility of sleep at Upton and prepares to leave the inn.

Frustrated in his search and angry at Tom, Western demands that he be tried for stealing Sophia's muff. A magistrate happens to be present in the inn, but since he does not have his clerk present nor his law books with him, he declines to try the case. Fitzpatrick, thereupon, offered to assist him, for he had indeed been articled to an attorney in Ireland for three years before crossing over to England and setting up in that walk of life which requires no apprenticeship, namely the business of being a "gentleman."

At first the case goes against Tom, but he is finally acquitted on the testimony of Partridge and Susan.

Tom and Partridge again take to the road, Western and his attendants including Parson Supple continue their search for Sophia, and Fitzpatrick and Maclachlan go by coach to Bath, finding room for Mrs. Waters, who becomes quite attached to Fitzpatrick and does all she can "to console him in the absence of his wife."

COMMENT: The Upton sequence begins in Book IX and runs through most of Book X. It represents, therefore, a major segment of the novel. The events at Upton are so numerous that it may be well to recapitulate before proceeding to comment.

1. Arrival of Tom at Upton with the half-naked woman he has rescued from Northerton.

2. The efforts of the landlord and landlady to oust Tom and his unprepossessing companion, precipitating a free-for-all.

3. Arrival, in a coach, of a young lady and her maid at the inn; the cessation of hostilities.

4. Arrival of a group of soldiers, with a deserter.

5. Recognition by the soldiers of Tom's companion as "Captain Waters' lady."

6. Mrs. Waters' seduction of Tom.

7. Revelation of some irregularity in Mrs. Waters' marriage and of her affair with Northerton.

8. Partridge's expression of his conviction that Tom is Squire Allworthy's son and heir.

9. A flashback to Tom's rescue of Mrs. Waters from Northerton. Having, as was revealed in Book VII, escaped from his confinement after nearly killing Tom, and believing he had killed Tom,

Northerton joined Mrs. Waters, whose "husband" had just left with his troops. She has money and valuables and Northerton was attempting to murder her for them when surprised by Tom.

10. The entrance of Fitzpatrick in pursuit of his wife.

11. Susan Chambermaid's mistaken belief that Mrs. Waters is Fitzpatrick's wife. The scuffle in her room, where Tom is encountered by Fitzpatrick.

12. The meeting between Maclachlan and Fitzpatrick.

13. The arrival of Sophia and Honour.

14. Partridge's disclosure of Tom's misconduct with Mrs. Waters.

15. Corroboration of Partridge's story and Sophia's pain and shock.

16. The incident of the muff.

17. Fitzpatrick's second frantic search for his wife.

18. The arrival of Squire Western.

19. The encounter between Western and Tom.

20. Departure from the inn.

Although the tone and action belong to the tradition of farce, there is an underlying seriousness to Fielding's many pungent comments on the action. Fitzpatrick, for example, is in part a stereotype, the "wild" Irishman of eighteenth century stage tradition. He is also a vehicle used by Fielding to call into question the value or profundity of his century's notion of what constituted a gentleman. The landlady, as another example, is a superbly realized comic figure. Fielding's ear for speech is, as usual, impeccable. But she also serves as a means of making a comment not only on landladies but on human nature in general. At one moment she si lambasting Tom, but when she believes that he is Squire Allworthy's son and heir she begins to sing a different tune.

As we have seen, Fielding can be bitingly anti-sentimental. One of the purposes of introducing into the story Tom's lapses from virtue is to emphasize this anti-sentimentality. In the sentimental tradition, true love would have protected Tom from tempation; in the actual world, flesh and blood are weak and can be persuaded to betray true love.

On the other hand, Fielding is not a cynic. He curiously combines disenchantment and realism with an infectious cheerfulness. He exhibits an exquisite sensibility in his treatment of Sophia. With admirable grace he traces her progress from loyal disbelief to disillusionment and pain. He understands her determination to hold her head high and preserve her self-respect. And the ambiguity of her gesture in depositing her muff in Tom's bed is masterly. Is this reproach or is she telling Tom that the muff no longer has any meaning for her and that she is discarding it and him forever?

The contrast between the sweetness and intelligence of Sophia (who is also spirited and adventuresome) and her brutal (but also in his own headstrong way loving) father is skillfully drawn. The comparison of Western's quest for his daughter with a fox hunt, a sport dear to the Squire's heart, arouses pity for Sophia and heightens our contempt for Western, but is at the same time amusing and contributes to the astonishing variety of this unflaggingly zestful story.

By way of summary, the reader of Fielding is advised to observe that Fielding is doing many things at once. He is fashioning a highly intricate plot, with an enormous number of incidents cunningly related to one another, and with the final outcome of the story carefully suppressed so that suspense will be built up; he is creating a large gallery of characters representative of various walks of life and occupations, some comical, some repulsive, some grotesque, some attractive; he is constantly chatting with his reader about what he is doing and about life in general; and he is, finally, commenting pointedly on topical problems of his age: the administration of justice and penological theory, the duties and obligations of parents and children, appearance and reality in the jealously preserved gradations in rank, marriage customs, habits of speech, the conditions of servants, game laws, and many others. Fielding wrote to please readers in general. He wrote with the conscience of an artist. He can, nevertheless, be profitably perused by historians and sociologists.

Fielding now turns backward in his history to tell of the events surrounding the escape of Sophia from her father's house. The morning of the scheduled wedding arrived, Blifil came to claim his bride, but Sophia was nowhere to be found. Mrs. Western accuses her brother for his interference in her bringing up of the girl; and the Squire, in turn, becomes angry with his supercilious and conceited sister. Blifil returns home, disappointed, but Square and Thwackum had taught him "to bear rather better than more passionate lovers bear these kinds of evils."

The night before Blifil's disappointment, Sophia and Honour had effected their planned escape. On horseback and with a guide, they set off for London, but decide to elude pursuit by following a circuitous route. In a conversation with the guide, Sophia learns only by chance the route that Tom had followed, and sets off after him. They keep on encountering people who had met Tom on his journey, and she is thus able to follow him to the inn at Upton.

BOOK XI

CONTAINING ABOUT THREE DAYS

In the introductory chapter Fielding continues to satirize captious and uninformed criticism, suggesting that some critics would rather condemn a book than praise it, that unjust criticism proceeds from ignorance of the love and effort that go into the making of a book, that there are even critics so malicious as to reject a book without reading it; that some criticism is much too general, and some too minutely particular, calling attention to minor faults in the work being criticized but ignoring the total impression made by it.

When the narrative proper resumes, Sophia, Honour, and their guide are again on horseback, speeding away from Upton. Before they had gone much more than a mile, they became conscious that other horses were behind them and they were terrified. When they are caught up, they are relieved to discover that the other party also consists of two women and a guide; in the dark and on the lonely road the two parties are happy to travel along together.

When it becomes light, the young ladies recognize one another. Sophia has been caught up with by her cousin Harriet, Fitzpatrick's runaway wife, who had left the inn at Upton only a few minutes after the departure of Sophia. The girls were not only cousins but also old and dear friends, having lived together for long periods of time with their aunt, Mrs. Western.

The parties ride on for many hours. Sophia, thoroughly exhausted by travel and having had little sleep for a couple of days, is in such condition as to make it imperative that they interrupt the journey to London at another inn.

While they rest, the landlord and landlady, with predictable and understandable curiosity, make inquires of the guides into the circumstances and stations of life of their new guests. Not altogether satisfied that the stories of the two guides are consistent, the landlord, who prides himself on his sagacity, comes up with the extravagant and utterly lunatic theory that Sophia is really Jenny Cameron, a Scottish girl reported to be loved by James, the Young Pretender to the English throne whose efforts to recover his throne were the sensation of the moment.

When Sophia and Harriet awoke, dressed, and had their tea, they considered setting out again toward London. But they were not especially anxious to face the perils and anxieties of another night on the road, and decided to spend the night at the inn. Had Sophia known of the arrival of her father at Upton, Fielding tells us, she might have been less willing to have delayed her journey; but, "as to Jones, she had," says Fielding, "I am afraid, no great horror at the thoughts of being overtaken by him; nay, to confess the truth, I believe she rather wished than feared it."

The cousins have not seen one another for some years. Harriet tells Sophia the story of her unhappy marriage. It seems that five years earlier she had been vacationing at Bath, the fashionable spa, with her Aunt Western. Here she met Fitzpatrick, a young man who was one of the gayest, handsomest, most gallant young blades at Bath that season.

Fitzpatrick, who, as the reader knows from the account given of him at the time of Tom's trial for the theft of Sophia's muff (Book X), is an upstart adventurer, first pays court to Mrs. Western. She, in her foolishness and blindness, is captivated by him, but gradually his attentions turn from aunt to niece. In spite of advice from those who could see into the unscrupulousness and opportunism of the young Irishman, Harriet was infatuated and married him. Her aunt was furious, left Bath abruptly, and terminated all connection with her niece.

Fitzpatrick now decided to return to Ireland, in spite of the remonstrations of Harriet and in spite of the fact that he had promised during his courtship that he would never insist on this journey against her will. A quarrel ensued. While her husband was out of the house, Harriet came upon a dunning letter addressed to her husband which made it abundantly clear that he had pursued both aunt and niece solely for "ready money."

Harriet proceeds to give Sophia a graphic account of her life in Ireland with her cynical, cruel, and avaricious husband, and of the rapid dissolution by his riotous living of the fortune that she brought him.

The story is interrupted by the entrance of the landlord, still under his curious misapprehension that Sophia is really Jenny Cameron.

Having heard that the rebels had won some successes, anxious to be on the winning side, he spoke to "Jenny" about recognizing her when she first arrived, about his great virtue in not having betrayed her, and about his expectation of reward. Poor Sophia hasn't the slightest notion of what most of his garbled discourse is about, but some of his phrases suggest to her that he is talking about her running away from her father. Honour is dispatched to find out just what the landlord and his household know.

Harriet's story continues. Her miseries with Fitzpatrick increased. She lost her only child. She learned that her husband was keeping a mistress. On an occasion when he returned and seemed to be all affection again, she discovered that he was badly in debt, wished to dispose of a piece of her property, and needed her signature. When she refused to sign, he confined her to her room. While he was away from home, however, she managed to escape and set out to seek protection from her brutish husband. While she was on this journey, she fell in with Sophia and decided to accompany her to London.

"Sophia now, at the desire of her cousin, related—not what follows, but what hath gone before in this history; for which reason the reader will, I suppose, excuse me for not repeating it over again. One remark, however, I cannot forbear making on her narrative, namely, that she made no more mention of Jones, from the beginning to the end, than if there had been no such person alive."

Honour returns to her mistress in a state of rage, having ascertained that the landlord thought that he was entertaining Jenny Cameron. Enraged at what she considers a blackening of Sophia's character, and feeling that she herself in her capacity as maid was besmirched by the landlord's suspicion, she has been engaged in one more of the lovely brawls that enliven the pages of *Tom Jones* and that provide Fielding with an opportunity to give full scope to his talent for the absurd and farcical and to exhibit his stylistic virtuosity, especially in the mock-heroic manner.

The arrival at the inn of "a great gentleman" is next announced, a man who asks permission to attend upon the ladies. Sophia is apprehensive, obviously fearful that it is her father who has caught up with them. But the man ushered into their room turns out to be an Irish peer, a neighbor of Harriet's in Ireland, who had befriended her and provided her with money for her elopement. Somehow Harriet had neglected to mention this gentleman or his kindness in her account of her life. Now she praises him highly to Sophia, dwelling upon the fact that he is one of the very few men of high rank who are faithful to their wives.

The next morning when Sophia, Harriet, their attendants, and the noble lord and his servants prepare to leave the inn, Sophia discovers that she has lost her money, the money her father had given her just before her running away when she had pleased him by pretending to be agreeable to his wishes.

The peer invites the hapless ladies to accompany him in his coach to London and they accept the invitation.

When, back in Somersetshire, Sophia had determined to avoid the hateful marriage with Blifil, she recollected that she had an acquaintance, a relative even, in London, who had in the past treated her with considerable kindness; and it was part of her plan to seek out her protection. Now arrived in London, she seeks her prospective benefactress, a certain Lady Bellaston, who turns out to be a lady very well known in the town. While getting herself settled in London, Sophia and Harriet share lodgings, but Sophia is shocked to learn that Harriet is secretly planning to meet her Irish peer at Bath; and Harriet, in turn, becomes somewhat petulant at what she considers the provincial morality of Sophia.

> **COMMENT:** The eleventh book represents the beginning of the final section of *Tom Jones*. It will be observed that the novel is divided into three large sections of unequal length: the first section has to do with Tom's boyhood and idyllic life in the country—idyllic, though not without its share of troubles and temptations; the second section could be called "On the Road." This section has not completely come to an end, for when Book XI concludes only Sophia and Harriet of the travellers have reached London; the third section is concerned with London life.
>
> The reader will observe how relentlessly Fielding is teasing him by the niggardly way in which he gives out information. Harriet Fitzpatrick, for example, at first enlists our sympathies. Married to a fortune-hunter who has squandered all of her estate, who has been unspeakably cruel, she seems a pathetic creature. But we gradually learn that she has not been completely honest with Sophia, that her own patterns of behavior are not above reproach, that she was headstrong when she married Fitzpatrick and resisted advice, that she plans to live according to the very loose code of the fashionable world, and that she has contempt for the principles of Sophia.

BOOK XII

AN ACCOUNT OF THE SAME THREE DAYS DESCRIBED IN BOOK XI

Ostensibly discussing the problem of plagiarism in modern literature, Fielding in the first chapter of this book actually discusses the proper use of tradition, allusion, quotation, comparison based on an educated author's familiarity with a body of literature that is part of the world's heritage, particularly with classical literature, and the traitorous stealing of the ideas and sentiments of a modern author.

The narrative now focuses on Western. Riding in pursuit of his daughter, he comes upon a fox hunt and cannot resist joining it. He loves Sophia but how can he be expected to miss an opportunity for a glorious chase after the hounds? "The squire who owned the hounds was highly pleased with the arrival of his brother squire and sportsman; for all men approve merit in their own way. . . ." After the hunt, Western, entertained by his "brother squire," became very drunk. On the following morning Parson Supple persuaded him to give up his search for Sophia and to return to his own home. Western, in an ugly mood, dispatched some of his attendants to continue the hunt for his daughter, but he goes back to his own estate.

Tom and Partridge, leaving the inn at Upton at about the same time as the Squire, are forced to travel again afoot since there are no horses available. Tom is in a state of despair, and Partridge hopefully once again tries to dissuade him from going on with his intention of joining the army.

They meet a beggar as they go on their way, and Tom, with characteristic generosity, gives the poor fellow a shilling. In return, the beggar offers to sell Tom a pocketbook that he has found on the road. In the book is Sophia's name, and also the money that she found that she had lost just while she was preparing to set out for London with her cousin Harriet. Overjoyed at his discovery, Tom gives the beggar a guinea for the book, but the beggar, realizing that he has turned over something of value to Tom although he, being unable to read, had not understood the value, demanded half of what the discovery was worth. Tom vainly tries to explain that the money is going to be returned to its rightful owner, and Partridge is forced to drive the beggar off. The journey continues.

Tom and Partridge next hear drums. Cowardly Partridge is frightened, certain that the Jacobite rebels are approaching, but Tom insists upon pressing on. They enter the next town and discover that a drum is being beaten only to announce a puppet-show. At the urging of Partridge, the two travellers dine and stay in town to see the puppet-show.

> **COMMENT:** The puppet-show incident is employed principally as a device for introducing Fielding's caustic observations on the tastes of his age. The puppet—show master, for example, remarks that "the present age was not improved in anything so much as in their puppet shows," which, if true, represents as devastating an observation as ever has been made on the eighteenth century. Even if not strictly true, the remark is illustrative of the bite and power of Fielding's satire.
>
> Fielding, continuing his irony, comments on the propriety of the entertainment provided by the puppet-show master, contrasting it with much "low" entertainment then coming into vogue. This amusing section is obviously partisan. There were people and critics in the eighteenth century who professed an absolute abhorrence of what they termed "the low." Samuel Johnson, in general a sensible and level-headed critic, complained of Shakespeare's using so low a term as "knife," a term, in Johnson's view, associated with the kitchen and therefore unfit for dignified poetry. Lord Chesterfield thought that laughter constituted an impropriety and urged his son never to exceed a polite smile. Fielding was in violent reaction against these extreme theories about the obligations of an educated and cultivated man, and vigorously fought the absurd critical doctrines on the "low."

After the show, the owner of it complacently and sanctimoniously speaks of the value of his art as a deterrent from vice. While he was going on in this way, one more uproarious incident in this uproarious novel broke out: the landlady of the inn at which Tom and Partridge had dined discovered her maid making love with one of the men in the puppet-show.

> **COMMENT:** This incident, furthering the element of farce in *Tom Jones,* is also very important in its relevance to Fielding's down-to-earth view of the relationship of art to life. It is one of the deepest convictions of man, not only of man in the eighteenth century but of man in every century, that art contributes to morality. There have always been skeptics. Plato in his *Republic* repudiated poets as the fashioners of pleasing fictions that misled youth and constituted a danger to the state.
>
> It would be a mistake on the foundation of an ironic and comic passage such as that just described, to rank Fielding among the skeptics. There are, indeed, good reasons for believing that Fielding is not only a novelist but also a moralist. But he is not

—and could not be—a humorless moralist, and he very well knew that mankind, whatever the intentions of its tutors, largely goes its own way.

Tom, who has had, in his travels, little sleep, is persuaded to pass the night in the local inn. With his bedfellows, the pocketbook and muff, he retires, but Partridge, who has managed many more naps on the journey, seeks the comforts of the kitchen—and there boasts to his companions about the fortune and high rank of his master. Increasingly disturbed at the way things are going, however, he describes Tom's frenetic behavior caused by unrequited love, and tries to get help in forcibly returning Tom to Allworthy's estate—confident that his action will bring a substantial reward from the benevolent Squire.

The company assembled in the kitchen is sympathetic but not anxious to run the risk of taking any direct action.

After his much-needed sleep, Tom wakes up, aroused by a violent battle going on near his room between the puppet-master and his clown (his Merry-Andrew). The clown is the member of the company that had been caught in dalliance with the innkeeper's servant. In the quarrel, he reminds his master that he has saved him from the gallows by stopping him from robbing and raping a beautiful girl they had encountered on the road.

Intervening in the quarrel, Tom discovers by inquiry that the girl was his beloved Sophia, and, ascertaining the direction she had taken, he and Partridge resume their pursuit.

A storm comes up and Tom and his companion once again take refuge in an inn. Here Tom meets the guide who had been with Sophia in her journey, and from him learns about the route that she has followed.

The guide, who is returning the horses that had been hired by Sophia, is, by money, persuaded by Tom to conduct them, on the horses, to the inn at which Sophia had last stopped. Tom thinks it no affront to his masculinity to ride side-saddle, even though the boy offers him the use of his own horse. Partridge, however, does feel that it is degrading for a man to ride side-saddle and accepts the boy's offer.

As they ride on, Partridge is very happy. He had thought that they were searching for the military unit in which Tom had enlisted, and he had no stomach for battle. Now he finally realizes that Tom is in quest of Sophia.

After four hours they reach the inn at which Sophia and Harriet had stayed. Tom asked for fresh horses but there were none to be had because of the coming and going that was caused by the excitement of the Jacobite rebellion. They are forced, therefore, to remain for a while at the inn.

There Tom is recognized and addressed by a man who turns out to be Dowling, the lawyer who had brought Blifil the news of his mother's death (Book V). Tom and Dowling sit down over a bottle of wine, and Tom gives Dowling an account of his life.

> **COMMENT:** The alert reader will suspect that Fielding has reasons for bringing Dowling back into the story. Of course, the conversation between Tom and Dowling provides the author with an opportunity to emphasize the selflessness of Tom by contrasting it with the crass practicality of Dowling, but one ought to wonder if there is not an additional reason for the re-introduction of a character who seems so minor.

Horses at last being available, Tom and Partridge leave the inn and take the road to Coventry. It is now night and it is raining, and the travelers lose their way. Partridge is certain that a witch has cast a spell upon them, and when his horse stumbles and he falls from it, he argues that this accident proves that he is right. Shortly after, their guide tumbles from his horse, and Partridge is thereby further convinced that they are bewitched.

> **COMMENT:** Witchcraft was scarcely the vital issue in the eighteenth century that it had been in the seventeenth century, but the memory of witch hunts was then fresher than now. And the introduction of the theme of witchcraft into the story was especially pertinent to the setting—the rebellion of 1745. James I, who had initiated the Stuart line in England, had been notoriously interested in witchcraft and demonology. James II, who had been driven from the throne which his grandson was now attempting to claim, was a Catholic, and, therefore, in eighteenth-century English eyes, superstitious. Partridge is represented as being a secret sympathizer with the Jacobite cause and a "Papist." It is, therefore, "logical" that he should be superstitious and a believer in witchcraft. He thus becomes a device whereby Fielding can express his own—and his century's—enlightened convictions.

The confused wayfarers spot a light in the distance, a light that intensifies Partridge's ludicrous terrors but which is welcome to the more sensible Tom. They press on, and meet with a band of gypsies, celebrating a wedding.

They join the feast. The king of the gypsies discusses with Tom the customs of his own people and the customs of Tom's. Partridge, in the meantime, having drunk too much, is tempted by a female gypsy and is discovered by the gypsy's husband in a compromising situation. A judicial inquiry reveals that the husband had witnessed the entire course of the flirtation and had not prevented it although he could have done so, and the king therefore rules that he is not entitled to the monetary amends that he had obviously been seeking.

> **COMMENT:** This, like the encounter with the Man of the Hill (Book VIII), is an episode—a story within the story told largely for its own sake but nonetheless related to the main story. It gives Fielding an opportunity to make some ironic reflections on the parochialism and smugness of his contemporaries, on justice, and on government. Particularly important are his reflections of absolutism, because of the background of the story. One reason for the expulsion of James II and for the general hatred of the Stuart family was the conviction, justified or not, that the Stuarts believed in the absolute prerogatives of kingship, in the "divine right of kings."

Still following the itinerary of Sophia but never catching up with her, Tom and Partridge proceed on their way to London. Partridge, knowing that Tom has Sophia's pocketbook, in which there is £100, remonstrates with him on his parsimoniousness. He thinks that they ought to dine more often and more sumptuously than they have been doing, Tom being especially indifferent to food. Tom is outraged by Partridge's disregard for honesty.

As they ride on, "a genteel-looking man but upon a very shabby horse" joins them. He says that he is apprehensive lest he be attacked by highwaymen. Tom replies that he has no such fears because he has very little to lose, whereupon Partridge reminds Tom that he has Sophio's banknote. The stranger then draws a pistol and demands the money. Tom offers him all of *his* money (three guineas), but the robber insists on having Sophia's. Tom, in spite of the pistol at his breast, grapples with the stranger and brings him to the ground. The defeated man begs for mercy, asserting that he has a wife and six children to support. Tom magnanimously lets him go without pressing charges, and as he and Partridge continue towards London, he comments on the barbarity of the English penal system.

> **COMMENT:** Fielding, as lawyer and magistrate, was keenly interested in the problem of justice and punishment. In the eighteenth century an extraordinary number of offenses were punishable by death, and executions ranked among the more popular of public spectacles. The highwayman of this section of the story will reappear, but for the time being it is perhaps best to stress the section as evidence of Fielding's humanitarianism.

BOOK XIII

TOM'S ARRIVAL IN LONDON

The first chapter is an elaborate invocation—to the love of fame and to the love of material rewards. It is deliberately stilted and thus amusing. In it, however, one can read some of Fielding's convictions about what a writer must have. He must have "genius," natural ability; "humanity," a feeling for people, compassion and understanding; "learning," an acquaintance with books, with the literary tradition; and he must have "experience," familiarity with the actualities of life.

Arriving in London, Jones is confused and it is only with the utmost difficulty that he finds his way to the town house of the Irish peer with whom, he had heard, Sophia and Harriet had gone to the metropolis. At last he finds the house but is told by the porter that there are no women staying there. The porter, however, reveals that he knows where the ladies are lodging and is persuaded by a bribe to conduct Tom there.

Tom unluckily arrives a few minutes after Sophia has gone out. Harriet's servant gives him this disappointing news but says that she cannot tell him where she has gone or when she will return. Tom had never seen Harriet but he had heard about the marriage of Sophia's cousin to a man named Fitzpatrick, and he presently realizes that his beloved is staying with her cousin. He asks to see her.

Harriet, however, thinks that Tom may be someone sent by Squire Western and she refuses to see him or give him any information about Sophia's whereabouts. Tom, however, makes such a favorable impression on Harriet's maid that she prevails upon her mistress to grant the young man an interview. When Tom appears in her presence she recognizes that this young man is in love with Sophia, but she mistakenly thinks that he is Blifil, from whom, as she knew, Sophia was running. Her maid, however, who had heard of Sophia's sentimental history from Honour and who therefore knew about Jones, suggested to her that the young man she had just seen was so attractive and well-mannered that he must be Jones rather than the odious Blifil. Harriet, of course, had never heard of Jones (Book XI, Chapter 8) but when she learns the omitted sections of Sophia's story she agrees with the maid, but decides that she still will be doing her cousin a favor if she protects her from so notorious a rake.

> **COMMENT:** In the light of her involvement with the Irish peer, Harriet's concern for Tom's reputation is ironic.

Fielding next makes it clear that there are practical considerations. Mrs. Fitzpatrick thinks that if she can keep Sophia from Tom and restore her to her father, Squire Western will be reconciled with her and will suitably reward her. So she visits Lady Bellaston, whose protection Sophia had gone to London to seek and with whom Sophia is now residing. Lady Bellaston refuses to have a part in sending Sophia back to her father, because she has heard from Mrs. Western that he is a brute. But she does agree to cooperate with Mrs. Fitzpatrick in keeping Sophia from Tom.

She exhibits unusual interest in Tom. She has already heard a great deal about him from her personal maid, Etoff, who has been listening to the gossip of Honour. Having heard that Tom was a handsome fellow, she was anxious to learn even more about him, and got as much further information as she could from Mrs. Fitzpatrick. She explains that she cannot very well deter Tom from seeing Sophia unless she can recognize him, and Harriet invites her to come to her lodgings in the evening when she expects to be visited again by Tom.

While this conversation goes on, Sophia is in her room with Honour and has not the slightest notion that Tom is so close by.

When Tom next arrives at Harriet's lodging, she asks to know why he wishes to see her cousin. Tom explains that he has a substantial sum of money to return to her. At this point they are interrupted by a violent knocking at the door, and Lady Bellaston, whose footman had been responsible for the knocking, sweeps into the room. There is an exchange of elaborate courtesies, and no sooner does the company get settled but what the Irish peer enters. Fielding ironically comments on the brilliance and elegance of the conversation that went on between the two fashionable women and the nobleman. Tom, a country boy, is baffled by it all and says hardly a thing.

It growing somewhat late, Mrs. Fitzgerald rather imperiously dismisses Tom without giving him an answer about whether or not she will arrange matters so that he can meet Sophia. She asks him to leave his address.

Lady Bellaston takes her leave shortly after Tom departs, and Harriet is left alone with her Irish peer.

> **COMMENT:** The reader can scarcely fail to notice that Fielding, for one reason or another, has emphasized Lady Bellaston's interest in Tom. He has also emphasized the treachery and duplicity of Harriet, and he continues to make broad insinuations about the nature of her relationship with her "protector."

It will already have been observed that Fielding spares no social class in this comprehensive satire. In this section, and throughout the rest of the novel, he holds up to ridicule the artificialities and affectations of fashionable society. Fielding was himself a gentleman but this did not prevent him from seeing the vices and follies of his own class.

On the next day Tom tries, in vain, several times to wait upon Mrs. Fitzpatrick, and he cannot understand why she is never at home to him. The reason, Fielding explains to the reader, is that the jealous Irish peer has forced her to promise not to see him again.

Tom had taken up lodgings in the home of a clergyman's widow, who has two daughters, Nancy, seventeen, and Betty, ten. He had applied for rooms for himself and Partridge in this house because he remembered that Allworthy was accustomed to using it on his visits to London.

After his fruitless attempts to see Mrs. Fitzpatrick, alone in his room and desolate, Tom hears an uproar in another part of the house and a female voice begging him to come and prevent a murder. Never slow to respond to appeals for help, Tom rushes to the scene and discovers the servant of another resident in the house chocking his master. Tom fights off the servant and is thanked by the gentleman and by the young lady with him, who proves to be Nancy, the elder daughter of the woman of the house. Tom and the rescued fellow-lodger share a bottle of wine and become friends, though Tom finds his new friend, whose name is Nightingale, a little tainted by the foppery of the town.

COMMENT: Nightingale is introduced so that Fielding can more easily build up the reader's suspense concerning the outcome of the main plot by directing attention to the adventures of Nightingale in a sub-plot (a plot related to the main plot but with an independent interest of its own). The presence of Nancy in Nightingale's room at the time of the fight arouses curiosity.

Nightingale is also a device whereby Fielding can elaborate his satire on London morals and manners. A pleasant enough fellow, he is a trifler—a man about town, an inveterate gambler, a coxcomb.

The fight between Nightingale and his servant throws some light on the relationship of servants and their employers in the age of Fielding. Nightingale unexpectedly returned home and found "four gentlemen of the cloth" (which does not mean, as a modern reader might expect it to, clergymen, but is, rather, a jocular way of saying "servants," an allusion to the fact that eighteenth-century servants, at least those of ladies and gentlemen, wore distinctive livery) playing cards in his room. They had spilled ale on Nightingale's dearest book, his Hoyle (the outstanding authority on card-games), and this so incensed him that he berated his servant and a ferocious fight followed. There are two points to observe: 1) that masters tended to be over-bearing and insolent toward servants; 2) that servants, on the other hand, were not always meek and submissive.

One further remark about the meeting with Nightingale: Tom's prowess is compared with the prowess of those trained in Mr. Broughton's school, at the time a kind of gymnasium where boxing was taught. We are reminded of the growing popularity of boxing among all classes, especially among the upper classes.

While Tom, Nightingale, Mrs. Miller (for so the mistress of the house was called), and her children are at breakfast the following morning, a porter arrives with a package for Tom. It contains a masquerade costume, a ticket, and a note that read:

> "The queen of the fairies sends you this;
> Use her favours not amiss."

Puzzled, Tom decides that the invitation must have come from Mrs. Fitzpatrick. The reader, of course, knows how unlikely this is, but Tom is of a naturally optimistic cast of mind and his hopes rise again.

Unhappily, by this time Tom had not one penny left in his pocket. "Notwithstanding, therefore, all the delicacies which love had set before him, namely, the hopes of seeing Sophia at the masquerade,—on which, however ill-founded his imagination might be, he had voluptuously feasted during the whole day,—the evening no sooner came than Mr. Jones began to languish for food of a grosser kind." In a word, he was hungry. Partridge suspects this, and once again advises him to return to Allworthy. Tom again explains to Partridge how mistaken is Partridge's belief that he is the Squire's son and heir and still in his good graces. Somewhat angry at the bewildered Partridge, he borrows a shilling from him, which is yielded very reluctantly because Partridge still believes that he should be using the banknote that belongs to Sophia. Tom sets off in a sedan chair, accompanied by Nightingale, for the masquerade.

Nightingale promptly leaves Tom to his own devices. Feverishly looking about the room for his Sophia, Tom is at length accosted by a masked lady who mentions Sophia's name to him; but on his entreaties to be led to her she assures him that she is not at the masquerade. Since the woman has mentioned Sophia, Tom can only believe that she is Mrs. Fitzpatrick and is disguising her voice. Their conversation continues and the lady becomes circumspectly but unmistakably flirtatious, and

Tom, always conscious of an obligation to be gallant, responds with his customary politeness. At length his masked companion announces that she has another engagement, and, begging Tom not to follow her in terms that suggest that she expects him to, she leaves in a chair (that is, a sedan chair, a mode of conveyance suitable for the narrow and winding streets of the eighteenth-century cities, carried by two men known as chairmen). Tom, penniless, follows her on foot, still hoping to learn of Sophia but not altogether unaware of the lady's true meaning.

Soon they find themselves alone in a well-furnished house. At Tom's request the lady unmasks; the fairy-queen turns out to be Lady Bellaston. The author, comically and suggestively, says that it would be tedious to give a circumstantial account of this tete-a-tete, but does, offhandedly, say that Tom spent the night.

COMMENT: Fielding could scarcely leave out of his account of London life a detailed description of a masquerade. For many years in the eighteenth-century this form of entertainment was all the rage, among the members of fashionable society and among those who sought the opportunity of mingling in fashionable society. Although masquerades were occasionally given in private homes, they were also a public form of entertainment, given in rooms rented for the purpose by men and sometimes by women who sold tickets for their own profit.

Although masquerades were extremely popular, there were not a few in England who had grave misgivings over the vogue. Some critics opposed them on social grounds, because they encouraged or at least permitted those of questionable social status to mingle with their "betters." Some opposed them on moral grounds and wondered darkly about the real purpose of disguise.

Throughout the passage Fielding employs innuendo, hints of none too subtle a nature, to suggest the profligacy of Lady Bellaston. At the masquerade, for example, she is remarkably skillful at recognizing people in spite of their disguises. Not only, in other words, is she an "old hand" at masquerades, but it would seem possible that she was on unusually intimate terms with the world of fashion.

The insistent irony of *Tom Jones* continues as our hero, seeking his beloved Sophia, finds himself entangled in the web of the spiderish Lady Bellaston. His fall is also occasioned by his gallantry and good-nature, two attractive characteristics but characteristics that can lead an impulsive and imprudent young man into difficulties.

Tom returns to his lodgings richer by £50 than when he set out. It seems that Lady Bellaston, though not usually conspicuous for her contributions to charitable institutions like hospitals, has seen fit to make a gift of a rather substantial amount of money to Tom.

On this day Tom and Nightingale are engaged to dine with the Miller family. The dinner is delayed two hours by the absence of Mrs. Miller.

When she at last appears she explains that she has been away visiting some destitute relatives, the Andersons, who are without the barest necessities of life and in the most pitiable of conditions. For one thing, they had never been very prudent, the parents having married for love rather than for money. For another thing, the father had been so unwise as put up security for his brother, and had lost everything through this generous but rash gesture.

Tom was so affected by Mrs. Miller's narrative that he immediately offered her his £50. She could not be prevailed upon to accept more than ten guineas (slightly more than one-fifth of the total), and expressed herself as overcome by Tom's generosity.

Nightingale was also touched but was notably more able than Tom to keep his head. First he belabored the obvious by complaining of the villanious behavior of the elder Anderson's brother; next he suggested that application be made to Allworthy (whom, of course, he had seen at Mrs. Miller's, where Allworthy stayed on his visits to London, and whose liberality would be known to him through Mrs. Miller); then he, not having been apprised of Tom's surreptitious gift, suggested a collection and offered himself to contribute the magnificent sum of a guinea.

COMMENT: The story of the Andersons introduced pathos into this variegated story, though not for the first time. We recollect Fielding's awareness of the plight of the Seagrim family after Black George's discharge from Allworthy's service.

Fielding's ability to sketch a graphic picture of poverty is certainly noteworthy, but perhaps even more important is his use of the Andersons in his exploration of the endlessly complicated problem of the nature of good and evil. Of all Tom's lapses from virtue, certainly the most shocking and offensive is his affair with Lady Bellaston. It will not do to say that he was simply once again the victim of the practiced arts of a worldly, experienced, and conscienceless woman. It will not do to say that he fell into her clutches only because he was desperate in his search for Sophia. It will not do to call attention to the hotness of young blood and the instinctive agreeableness of this passionate young man. At this point in the story Tom has become a kept man.

Yet immediately after the revelation of this fact we find him spontaneously offering all that Lady Bellaston has given him to relieve the wants of a family he does not even know, prompted only by his ready sympathy and total unselfishness.

The discussions of love and prudence that attend Mrs. Miller's account of the Andersons look back toward other discussions of love as it exhibits itself in the society that Fielding is writing about; and the alert reader, prepared to suspect that Fielding is foreshadowing events, wonders precisely what events that follow will be related to this discussion. It does not take much acumen to sense that something is going on between Nancy Miller and Nightingale.

Tom's unhappy affair with Lady Bellaston continues. She is lavish in her gifts, but Tom increasingly despairs of ever winning Sophia. First, he has no reason to disbelieve Lady Bellaston's assurances that Sophia wants to have nothing more to do with him; second, he is unwilling to expose Sophia to the danger of being disinherited from her father's estate—"the almost inevitable consequence of their coming together without a consent which he had no hopes of ever obtaining . . ." Third, he was conscious of his obligations to Lady Bellaston, by whose means he "was now become one of the best-dressed men about town."

After much reflection, he decides that although he loves Sophia and is less than enchanted with the autumnal charms of his benefactress, he had best face up to things as they are and stay with Lady Bellaston.

While still meditating on these matters, two letters arrive from Lady Bellaston in rapid succession. One tells him that circumstances make an appointed meeting impossible; the second tells him that other circumstances suggest that Tom dine with her in her own home—where, of course, the presence of Sophia and Honour pose practical difficulties to the lustful Lady.

Tom had been glad that his appointment with his aggressive inamorata had been called off, because he was looking forward to a night at the theatre with Nightingale. He was, accordingly, disappointed when the second note arrived.

The first of the two letters had been prompted by the fact that since their first meeting Tom and Lady Bellaston had been trysting in the home of a lady, one under some obligations to Lady Bellaston, who had recently turned Methodist and who henceforth refused to allow her house to be used for immoral purposes. The indomitable Lady Bellaston, however, after dispatching the first of the two notes, thought things over and decided to take a chance and arrange a meeting, for the first time, in her own home. She thereupon proposed that Sophia, Honour, and her own personal maid, Mrs. Etoff, attend a play.

When Tom has just completed dressing for his meeting with Lady Bellaston, Mrs. Miller raps on his door and invites him to her rooms. Here she presents him to her visitor, her poor relation, Anderson, whose need Tom's generosity has relieved and who has come to thank him in person. Tom is startled because Anderson proves to be the ineffectual highwayman who had made such a botch of robbing Tom (concluding section of Book XII), but he gracefully conceals the fact that they have met before. Tom acknowledges the professions of gratitude of Anderson and hurries off to his appointment.

He is in Lady Bellaston's drawing-room for only a few minutes when Sophia bursts in, expecting to find the room empty because her hostess had told her that she was going to be out for the evening. Lady Bellaston has not yet come to the drawing-room. Thinking she was alone, Sophia approaches a mirror, and then comes the discovery of Tom. A pathetic and not altogether unamusing scene follows, especially after the arrival of Lady Bellaston into the room.

Sophia's unexpected return from the playhouse had been occasioned by a riot that had broken out there between the adherents of the author and those who had banded together to make fun of his play. All the actors in the sentimental and comic scene in Lady Bellaston's drawing-room act out their parts to their own satisfaction. Tom pretends that he has only called to return Sophia's lost pocketbook, whose owner he was able to track down because of the name written in it; Sophia pretends that she has never before seen the fellow who has given her back her lost money; Lady Bellaston pretends that she is taken in by the whole farce. On his way out Tom meets Honour and gives her his address so that Sophia will know where he is lodging. After the departure of Tom, however, she torments Sophia with ambiguities.

COMMENT: Fielding's exceedingly delicate and subtle foreshadowing is illustrated in this section. Tom is (ironically, because, as events turn out, he is about, at long last, to meet Sophia again) vexed at having to attend upon Lady Bellaston; he had been looking forward to going to the theatre, having heard rumors that things there on this particular night would be lively.

The rumors were accurate. Things were lively—and Sophia thought it prudent to leave, thus walking into a somewhat awkward situation, but well before it had become too awkward. The encounter between Tom, Sophia, and Lady Bellaston is so managed as to make a reader suspect (if he did not know it) that Fielding had had some experience in (or at least had some talent for) writing for the stage.

It perhaps should be remarked that riots in playhouses were not uncommon in the robust English eighteenth century, and that Fielding, as playwright and manager, would have been thoroughly familiar with them.

BOOK XIV

MORE INFORMATION ABOUT MRS. MILLER AND THE CONTINUATION OF NIGHTINGALE'S ADVENTURES

The introductory chapter is, characteristically, satirical, and satirical in the usual two-edged fashion of Fielding. He complains about authors who presume to write about the fashionable world when they know nothing whatsoever about it; he also says that the fashionable world is much duller than the "ordinary" world. Behind all of this is Fielding's sensible conviction that a writer ought to know what he is writing about, that the knowledge can come only from experience and not from books, and that, furthermore, we all are the victims of our delusions.

Anxious and confused letters from Lady Bellaston follow. She is angry at Tom because of his affection for Sophia. Then she is willing to forgive him if he will visit her. Before he can obey the summons, the distraught and aging Lady appears at Tom's lodging. She has scarcely got into Tom's room when Partridge capers in triumphantly announcing the sudden and, to him, unexpected arrival of Mrs. Honour. Tom hides Lady Bellaston behind his bed as Honor enters with a letter from Sophia. Ignorant of the fact that Lady Bellaston is in the room, Honour launches forth into a denunciation of the Lady, in spite of Tom's efforts to silence her.

Honour finally leaves and Lady Bellaston emerges from her hiding-place, furious at all that she has heard, and especially venomous toward her rival, a mere "country girl . . . an idiot." She demands to see the letter that Honour has delivered, but Tom refuses, in spite of the remonstrances of Lady Bellaston, to be so dishonorable as to show it. Lady Bellaston recognizes that Tom's sense of honor is too much for her, and ceases her demands. She suggests, however, that he continue his visits to her house under the pretext that he is visiting Sophia.

After the departure of Lady Bellaston, Tom, with infinite relief, tears open her letter and reads it. He learns that Sophia is not a little suspicious of Lady Bellaston's integrity and fears that she is quite capable of betraying her to her father. She therefore begs Tom not to call on her again.

Tom decides that the best thing he can do is to pretend to be ill, and to communicate this news to both ladies.

Insatiable Lady Bellaston sends him a letter in return, announcing that she intends to visit him that evening in his lodgings, and warns him to arrange things so that there will be no complications.

After he receives this peremptory note, Tom is visited by Mrs. Miller, who complains about his entertaining women in her house and thus damaging the reputation of herself and her daughter. Tom tries to explain that his visitor (i.e., Lady Bellaston) was one of his "near" relations, but Mrs. Miller thinks that Tom's visitor departed at a very unconventional hour (about 2 A.M.) and had, furthermore, been somewhat agitated by some cynical and coarse remarks by Partridge. She proceeds to announce that she now sees the justice of Mr. Allworthy's observations of him. She was prepared to believe better of him because of his conduct toward the Andersons, but she worries about her daughters.

Moved by the reference to Allworthy, Tom offers to seek for other lodgings.

Mrs. Miller leaves and Nightingale enters, teases Tom on his recent visitors, and says that he is anxious to find lodgings in some other part of town. The two friends exchange confidences and it is revealed that Nightingale and Nancy are lovers. It also comes out that Nightingale's father has planned for him a marriage with an heiress, and it is for this reason that Nightingale wishes to quit the Miller household.

> **COMMENT:** The scene in Tom's bedroom with Lady Bellaston and Honour is farcical. After the departure of Honour, the altercation with Lady Bellaston is partly farcical but is also a means of showing that Tom, for all of his being kept by Lady Bellaston, is capable of moral judgment.
>
> The apprehensions of Mrs. Miller are natural and are evidence of her maternal conscientiousness. They also provide a way of getting Squire Allworthy back into the reader's consciousness. And Tom's honorable decision to leave Mrs. Miller's leads to the further development of the story of Nightingale's romance, specifically to the explanation of the difficulties that face the lovers because of such things as parental greed and a general ignorance of the nature of true love.

Somewhat later, Mrs. Miller invites Tom to join her at tea. Although she had protested his having female visitors in his room at odd hours, she retained some affection for him because of his exceptional goodheartedness and because of his connection with Squire Allworthy.

She tells Tom how good Allworthy has been to her. When she was widowed, he had established her in this London house and had settled an annuity on her. Although word of Allworthy's displeasure with Tom had reached her ears, she assures him that she has often heard the Squire speak affectionately of him, and she begs Tom to be more prudent in the future.

Tom repays Mrs. Miller's confidences by narrating his own history, but in the course of it never once mentions the name of Sophia. He also explains to his landlady that he was obliged once more to receive a lady in his room, but promises that this would be the last time. He said that his visitor was "one of great distinction" and that "nothing but what was entirely innocent was to pass between them." Fielding drily intervenes in the story to remark: "And I do firmly believe he intended to keep his word."

Tom returns to his room and waits, but Lady Bellaston's promised visit fails to materialize.

Tom falls asleep, with his thoughts not on Lady Bellaston but on Nancy Miller and Nightingale and their apparently insoluble problems. He awakens the next morning to find the house in an uproar. He discovers that Mrs. Miller has learned that her daughter is pregnant, and that Nightingale has sent her a letter explaining that he is obliged to marry the woman of his father's choice since he is himself penniless. In her despair, Nancy has twice attempted to destroy herself. Tom, profoundly moved by this turn of events, tries to comfort the Millers and promises to take more direct action. He goes to visit Nightingale, who has taken new lodgings.

The interview between Tom and his friend is not altogether successful. Acknowledging the force of Tom's eloquent championship of Nancy and of the rules of honor, Nightingale pleads his helplessness. He has no money and therefore cannot oppose the will of his father, who has, incidentally, arranged a meeting between his son and the heiress he wants for him on the following day. Tom, nothing daunted, proposes to reason with Nightingale's obdurate father.

He arrives at the elder Nightingale's lodging immediately after that gentleman had completed the arrangements for the marriage. At first Mr. Nightingale was suspicious that Tom was one of the young sparks with whom his son associated, and was afraid that Tom had come to claim a debt. When he learned that his suspicions were unfounded, he unbent a little and listened to Tom's arguments. Getting nowhere, Tom at last resorted to a kind of subterfuge and told the father that young Jack Nightingale was married. Before Mr. Nightingale could recover from this blow, a gentleman came into the room and greeted him as "brother." This other Nightingale has come to dissuade his brother from going through with his plans to marry off his son to the heiress, Miss Harris, and is delighted when he learns of Jack's marriage to

Nancy Miller. Tom is delighted that he has found an ally, and persuades Jack's uncle to return with him to the Miller household, where young Nightingale had promised to meet him.

While he has been gone, Nightingale has thought better of his abandonment of Nancy, and has determined to marry her in spite of his father's objections. When Tom and the uncle arrive and the uncle congratulates the happy pair on their "marriage," announced by Tom, they become flustered and the uncle becomes suspicious. The old gentleman proceeds to take advantage of the happy occasion in the Miller house and to get his nephew somewhat drunk. Uncle and nephew repair to Jack Nightingale's old rooms in the Miller's, and the uncle wrings a confession from Jack that he is not actually married. The uncle urges Jack to break off his engagement and, sensing that his arguments are not persuasive, he invites his nephew to accompany him to his own lodgings. Jack is not so drunk that he cannot whisper, on his way out of the house, to Nancy that he will join her in the morning and carry out his promises.

Tom, however, does not like the way things are going. He thinks that this carrying off of the bridegroom the night before the wedding is more than passing strange. But while he is still reflecting on these matters, Honour enters, bearing "dreadful news concerning his Sophia," and here the fourteenth book comes to an end.

> **COMMENT:** Although attention is focused on the misfortunes of Tom's friend, Nightingale, Tom himself, nevertheless, is very much in the forefront of the action, and the Tom that we see is the attractive and virtuous "hero" of the "history." Not only does the author explicitly describe Tom's good qualities, but he also dramatizes them by showing them as they appear against the weakness of Nightingale, the avarice of Nightingale's father, and the complete lack of principles of his uncle.
>
> The pungency of Fielding's style reveals itself in such passages as these:
>
> > "In fact, poor Jones was one of the best-natured fellows alive, and had all that weakness which is called compassion, and which distinguishes this imperfect character from that noble firmness of mind which rolls a man, as it were, within himself, and, like a polished bowl, enables him to run through the world without being once stopped by the calamities which happen to others."
> >
> > "This gentleman [Nightingale's father] . . . was what they call a man of the world; that is to say, a man who directs his conduct in this world as one who, being fully

> persuaded there is no other, is resolved to make the most of this. . . . He had . . . conversed so entirely with money, that it may be almost doubted whether he imagined whether there was any other thing really existing in the world; this at least may be certainly averred, that he firmly believed nothing else to have any real value."

BOOK XV

IN WHICH THE HISTORY ADVANCES ABOUT TWO DAYS

In the first chapter, which pretends not to be a preface on the ground that the book is too short to need a preface, Fielding makes at least two of his most important statements concerning his ethical position. First, he utterly rejects the speciously optimistic view of morality. "There are a set of religious, or rather moral writers, who teach that virtue is the certain road to happiness, and vice to misery, in this world. A very wholesome and comfortable doctrine, and to which we have but one objection, namely, that it is not true." Secondly, he rejects the notion that virtue can be examined apart from man's nature as a social animal. "But if by virtue is meant (as I almost think it ought) a certain relative quality which is always busying itself without-doors, and seems as much interested in pursuing the good of others as its own, I cannot . . . agree that this is the surest way to human happiness," because in this imperfect world those who are kind and benevolent are often abused for their pains.

As this book opens the author asks us to retrace our steps to that moment in the story when Sophia unexpectedly returned from the playhouse. It seems that when, in her fright, she had left the theatre, she had been escorted home by a young gallant who was acquainted with Lady Bellaston. He was much taken with Sophia and called upon her on the following day. His visit suggested to the madly jealous Lady Bellaston "a very black design against Sophia." She decides to encourage the young gallant, a nobleman named Lord Fellamar, to press his suit by telling him about Sophia's fortune and by warning him that she is in love with "one of the lowest fellows in the world," a bastard and a beggar. She goes so far as to suggest, in delicate but unmistakable terms, that he assure his success by raping Sophia.

To make Fellamar see that Sophia is in love with Jones and that haste and forceful action are absolutely necessary, Lady Bellaston concocts a story about Tom's being killed in a duel. One of her dissolute friends, at her bidding, relates the story at a gathering that included Sophia. She is, of course, visibly affected, and his lordship is convinced.

Before he puts into execution the evil instructions of Lady Bellaston,

Fellamar is overcome with scruples, approaches his unprincipled friend and announces his withdrawal from the scheme. She overcomes his scruples, however, by reminding him of the fortune that Sophia is certain to inherit, and he again agrees to rape Sophia.

COMMENT: The prologue that pretends to be no prologue is one more example of Fielding's artful foreshadowing. When he comments on the fact that people who actively concern themselves with the welfare of their fellows often, ironically, suffer for their virtue, he anticipates some of the things that are about to befall Tom Jones.

Lady Bellaston's planted lie about Tom's duel is still another interesting hint of what is to come, as soon be seen.

There was never any doubt about the odiousness of Lady Bellaston, but in her advice to Lord Fellamar she proves herself an absolute monster—almost too monstrous to be believable, but it is one of the noteworthy facts about Fielding that he uses realism only when it seems to him to serve his purpose. He has no objection to exaggeration, the excessive use of coincidence, wild improbability. He reflects the England of his day but he simultaneously is busy creating his own world. To put it another way, the landscape of *Tom Jones* is remarkably like the landscape of eighteenth-century England, but should not be confused with it.

Lord Fellamar's polished manners and brutish instincts add another dimension to Fielding's remorseless exposure of the so-called upper classes of fashionable London.

An opportunity having been provided, Lord Fellamar arrives at Lady Bellaston's and finds Sophia alone. While he is attempting to take possession of her by force, Squire Western and his attendants noisily enter the house. Fellamar, naturally, desists, having only slightly disarrayed his intended victim. Western and his party burst into the room and the Squire, drunk and speaking broad Somersetshire dialect, berates his "undutiful" daughter. Parson Supple begins to intercede for the poor frightened girl but stops at once at Western's ill-concealed hint that such intercession could cost him his church benefices.

Lady Bellaston is drawn to the room by the tumult, and Western plaintively accuses his daughter of hankering after a beggarly rascal when she might "marry one of the greatest matches in all England." Knowing nothing of Blifil, Fellamar in his self-conceit thinks that he is meant and steps forward to pay his respects to the Squire. The drunken, rowdy Western, offended by Fellamar's dandyism, calls him a "son of a b———." His lordship is bitterly resentful but disdains to create a scene before ladies and haughtily withdraws from the room.

Western now takes Sophia away from Lady Bellaston's. When Honour offers to accompany her mistress, he, angry at her having been an accomplice, roughly pushes her away and tells her that she has been discharged.
Fielding now pauses to explain how the squire discovered the whereabouts of his daughter. Harriet Fitzpatrick, anxious to be reconciled to her uncle and aunt, wrote Mrs. Western a letter divulging the fact that Sophia was living in Lady Bellaston's town-house. Western was overjoyed at the news and prepared to go at once to London. Mrs. Western warns her brother that he does not understand London ways and had best leave negotiations to an experienced "politician" like herself. They quarrel, eventually making up, and the Squire leaves to recover his daughter, his sister announcing her intention to visit London, too.

Fielding now brings us back to Tom Jones at the moment when Honour arrived at Mrs. Miller's, bearing "dreadful news." While she is narrating (in Tom's room, where they had repaired for privacy) the foregoing events, Partridge comes in to tell Tom that Lady Bellaston is approaching. Tom is terribly upset because Honour knows nothing of his connection with Lady Bellaston, but in his confusion he chooses the worst possible course of action: he hides Honour in a curtained recess behind his bed.

> **COMMENT:** It is instructive to observe with what extraordinary artistic economy Fielding uses his characters for various purposes. Squire Western, for example, is a comic character with his Somersetshire dialect, his uncouthness, his vulgarity; he is also a symbol of tyranny and brutality. Lord Fellamar, as a spineless and greedy accomplice of Lady Bellaston, is an ugly figure, a villain; he also serves Fielding's satire on the superficiality of fashionable life.
>
> It is also instructive to note Fielding's remarkable knowledge of how human beings act. Tom's befuddlement on the occasion of Honour's approach is a prime example. He could readily have explained to Lady Bellaston why Honour was in his room, for Honour had been staying with Sophia at Lady Bellaston's and nothing could have been more natural than her coming to acquaint Tom with Western's rediscovery of his daughter. But Tom, in typically human fashion, lost his head and committed the folly of hiding Honour—in a place where she was certain to learn of Tom's relationship with Lady Bellaston and thus be in a position, if opportunity should offer, to add to the bill of particulars in the charge against our hero.

Lady Bellaston, as was to have been expected, behaves provocatively and fails to understand why Tom, who is beside himself with embarrassment, does not respond to her encouragement. He is, as it were, rescued from his predicament by the sudden arrival of Nightingale, "dead drunk." Before Nightingale can actually enter the room (which he has mistaken for his own old room), Tom leaps up, meets his friend, and guides him to his own bed.

Apprehensive lest the drunken Nightingale wander back and discover her, Lady Bellaston, remembering the hiding-place behind Tom's bed (see the beginning of Book XIV) betakes herself there and comes upon Honour. There is a squabble, but the calculating Lady Bellaston thinks to herself that she can use the friendship of Honour and offers her a position in her household. Tom comes back to the room, worried, but Lady Bellaston imperiously sweeps out.

The reader must be wondering how Nightingale got away from his uncle. It seems that the uncle had a marriageable daughter and hoped that she might marry her cousin Jack. But while he is plying Jack with drink and thus detaining him from his intention of marrying Nancy Miller, a messenger brings the news that his daughter had eloped with a young clergyman, whose only disqualification was that he had no money. Angry and agitated, the uncle rushed off, "scarce knowing what he did, nor whither he went."

Nightingale was thus able, though drunk, to return to the Millers, sleep, and on the following morning take Nancy as his wife.

When Tom returns to his room after the wedding he receives, in succession, three frantic letters from Lady Bellaston, imploring him to visit her. Nightingale is with him at the time and chaffs him about Lady Bellaston, for everyone in the house knows who Tom's "visitor" is. At first, in gentlemanly fashion, Tom pretends that he does not know who Lady Bellaston is, but Nightingale laughs and tells Tom of her notoriety. Tom is genuinely shocked. He has never been very happy about his involvement with her ladyship but has felt hopelessly trapped. Now he longs for release. Nightingale tells him to propose marriage. One of her former lovers had proposed marriage and had been instantly dismissed.

Tom was persuaded to try the experiment, and sent Lady Bellaston a written proposal. He received in return an indignant reply in which Lady Bellaston ridiculed marriage, questioned his motives—but invited him to visit her again that evening.

Taking advice from Nightingale, Tom writes an amusing letter explaining that he can no longer take the risk of sullying her ladyship's reputation by carrying on an illicit affair, and, with remarkable tact and in the language of high compliment, announces that he is regretfully giving her up, hoping to return his "pecuniary obligations" and ever mindful of obligations "of a more tender kind." Whatever the style, a rebuff is a rebuff. Lady Bellaston wrote back: "I see you are a villain! and I despise you from my soul. If you come here I shall not be at home."

COMMENT: It would seem that Tom has at last freed himself from Lady Bellaston; but in Fielding, as in life, actions have consequences, and the reader may legitimately be curious as to the relationship of this shabby and sordid affair of Tom's to his future life.

Lady Bellaston's cynical attitude toward marriage as expressed in her somewhat ambivalent letter to Tom after his proposal—she speaks of "that monstrous animal a husband and wife"—draws attention to a conflict, in the eighteenth century (though the conflict reveals itself in various forms in other centuries), between what can be called "bourgeois" morality and "aristocratic" morality.

The wedding dinner is served and at its conclusion a letter is delivered to Mrs. Miller. From Allworthy, it announced his intention of coming to town with his nephew Blifil and requested accommodations at Mrs. Miller's. This means, of course, that Tom and the newly-married couple must take themselves to new lodgings. Tom was disturbed because he had given his address to Honour (end of Book XIII) and has had no recent news from her about Sophia. In the midst of his anxiety, a letter from Mrs. Honour is brought him, in which the faithless maid explains that she is now employed by Lady Bellaston and can be of no further service to Tom.

Fortune has further blows in store for our hero who has already been mightily tried. A very wealthy widow, a friend of Mrs. Miller, who has seen Tom and been mightily impressed by his handsomeness and gallantry, presumes to send him a letter containing a proposal of marriage. Tom, again penniless and without prospects, was tempted—but on this occasion he resisted temptation and gracefully but firmly turned down the offer of Arabella Hunt..

While Tom was still exulting over his triumphant conquest of temptation, Partridge entered with the news that Black George was with Squire Western's party. Tom learns that Western and Sophia are residing not many streets away. He prepares to write a letter to Sophia which can be delivered to her by Black George, who can be found by Partridge.

COMMENT: The forthcoming arrival of Allworthy and Blifii is, in effect, an announcement that the story is now moving toward its conclusion. But Fielding has so cunningly manipulated his plot that it is well-nigh impossible to decide exactly what will happen next. Tom is very far from the attainment of his desires. Sophia clearly loves him, but she is still, understandably, angry at him. She is also very much the captive of her father.

To turn from plot to details, the letter from Honour to Tom is notable for its comic misspellings. It is unlikely that Fielding meant to be cruel toward people who had not had the advantages of a good education. It is, rather, likely that he wished to contrast Honour's airs with her actual accomplishments.

The letter from Arabella Hunt has *some* connection with the plot (it is one more temptation for Tom), but it exists largely to provide Fielding with an opportunity to make some sardonic comments on women, widows, amorousness, and the facile consolations of religion. It is perhaps best appreciated as a kind of comic commentary on St. Paul's famous observation that "it is better to marry than burn."

BOOK XVI

NEW HOPES, NEW DESPAIRS

The first chapter is a discussion of Fielding's first chapters. They were suggested to him by the contemporary practice of opening plays with prologues. As Fielding's readers must know, prologues "seem all to be written on the same three topics, viz. an abuse of the taste of the town, a condemnation of all contemporary authors, and an eulogium on the performance just about to be represented." They have, in other words, no organic connection with the play to which they are prefixed. Accordingly, Fielding's readers should not expect that his initial chapters will have any special relationship to the book they introduce.

He goes on to say, sardonically, that prologues have one advantage: they give the critic something "that may serve as a whetstone to his noble spirit"; they give him an opportunity "to try his faculty of hissing."

Fielding's first chapters have still another advantage: those of his readers who are pressed for time can omit the first few pages of each of the eighteen books!

COMMENT: As usual, Fielding is both to be believed and not to be believed. He is right in saying that his first chapters have no necessary connection with the book they introduce (as this first chapter itself so well demonstrates). On the other hand, taken altogether the first chapters are very important for our understanding of the style and purpose of *Tom Jones,* and even though they are jocular they give valuable insights into Fielding's view of the relationship that exists between life and literature.

It should further be remarked that Fielding ought to be taken seriously as a literary critic. In this first chapter he pillories the stale, platitudinous prologues that introduced eighteenth-century plays. There were some very good prologues. In an earlier generation Dryden had done much to establish his reputation as a poet and wit by his fresh, amusing and challenging prologues and epilogues. In Fielding's own time, David Garrick, the greatest of eighteenth-century men of the theatre (actor, playwright, adapter, manager), wrote excellent prologues. For the most part, however, there was a dreary sameness about the prologues Fielding knew, and he quite properly attacks them with his incisive satiric pen.

He also in this short but brilliant chapter again strikes out at the malevolence of critics. It is not that a critic has no right to condemn a poem, a play, a novel—whatever he is scrutinizing—but rather Fielding's point is that too many critics think that their only task is condemnation. Too many critics approach a work pre-determined to dislike it.

Finally, Fielding ironically comments on the laziness of readers, and pretends to be their benefactor by sparing them the pains of reading several pages of his book. The truth of the matter is that the first chapters of the books into which *Tom Jones* is divided are an essential part of the novel.

Sophia, having been conveyed by her father to his lodgings, is steadfast in her determination not to marry Blifil. Her father, therefore, locks her in her room, and swears that she will not be released from her confinement until she obeys him.

Two days later, when he and Parson Supple were drinking their breakfast, a visitor was announced. An elegant gentleman is then ushered in, and he transmits a formal proposal of marriage from Lord Fellamar. Western scarcely understands the pretentiously phrased proposal, but grasps enough of it to know what it is, and tells the emissary that his daughter has already been spoken for. Fellamar's friend, thereupon, issues, again in ceremonious language, a challenge to a duel in Hyde Park. Western, who cares not a whit for the elaborate code of etiquette that governs fashionable life, contemptuously dismisses the challenge by saying that he is too busy. His visitor remonstrates, saying that his lordship's "honour will not suffer his putting up such an indignity as you must be sensible you offered him." The Squire replies that "it is a d——n'd lie," that he has never offered Fellamar anything. Fellamar's representative, resenting the word "lie," beats Western with his walking-stick, and a lively skirmish takes place. Western's complete ignorance of "manners" is so palpable that his adversary, a captain in the army, retires in disgust, saying, "I see, sir, you are below my notice" and promising to inform his lordship that the Squire is also below his.

Sophia, hearing the scuffle, cries out and beats on the door of her room.

After the departure of the captain, Western went to his daughter, "whom he loved so tenderly, that the least apprehension of any harm happening to her threw him presently into agonies." For all of his tenderness, he is vehement in his demands that she marry Blifil, and she, for all of her dutifulness, remains determined not to marry a man she finds detestable.

Black George delivers a meal to Sophia. At first she refuses it but the gamekeeper suggests to her that she will find some interesting delicacies, "eggs," in the chicken he has brought her. When George departs and her father again locks her door, she finds a letter from Tom. It is a rapturous love-letter in which he begs her to fly to his arms but not if, on mature consideration, she considers the sacrifice she would have to make too great, for Tom is only concerned with her happiness and welfare. "What Sophia said, or did, or thought, upon this letter, how often she read it, or whether more than once, shall all be left to our reader's imagination. The answer to it he may perhaps see hereafter, but not at present: for this reason, among others, that she did not now write any, and that for several good causes, one of which was this, she had no paper, pen, nor ink."

While meditating upon Tom's letter, Sophia hears a violent argument in another part of the house and recognizes the "shriller pipes" as the voice of her Aunt Western.

Mrs. Western, having come up to town, as she has promised that she was going to do, is now complaining that her brother has taken most unfashionable lodgings and is completely mismanaging his daughter's affairs. Balky and angry as he is, Western knows that he is the stipulated heir of his sister's considerable fortune and that "the bitch can't live for ever," and therefore grudgingly yields to her demands. He turns over to her the keys to Sophia's room and allows her to take Sophia to her own more agreeable quarters.

COMMENT: Mrs. Western is essentially a comic and grotesque figure. She is also a passionate spokesman for the rights of women, an eighteenth-century feminist. "Have I not often told you," she says to her brother, "that women in a free country are not to be treated with . . . arbitrary power?" It should not be thought that the feminist movement was in its infancy in Fielding's day. Chaucer's Wife of Bath was, centuries before, an eloquent champion of women's rights and a convinced believer in the innate superiority of women. There may, however, be something worth reflecting upon in the fact that until the triumph in the twentieth century of the suffragist cause, outspoken feminists were usually treated as comic characters.

In the section of the novel just described, Parson Supple's sycophancy is touched upon in various ways. Fielding's ethical convictions, though not systematic (how could they be in novels?) or totally coherent, are reasonably clear. His positive beliefs about religion are not clear, but it is easy to see what he opposes. The dependence of the clergy on patronage is an historic fact; Fielding also sees it as a great wrong.

Before departing with Sophia, Mrs. Western tells her brother that before she had set out for London, "that impudent fellow with the odious Irish name—that Fitzpatrick" had broken in upon her and had told her a rambling and unintelligible tale about his wife. She deports that she had then given him the letter Harriet had written, betraying Sophia, and told him that he could answer it himself. She assured her brother that she intended to have nothing more to do with Harriet (by whose bad example she was confident Sophia would profit), and he agrred that he, too, would not forgive his niece.

Sophia, restored to liberty, dispatches, by means of Black George, a letter to Tom, announcing the change in her situation but explaining that she "will not see or converse with any person" without her aunt's consent and that, accordingly, even though her aunt had not specified that she should not write letters, she feels obliged to tell Tom that she will not write to him again. She encloses in the letter the £ 100 banknote Tom had returned to her, because she is conscious that he is in need, but she urges him not to write to her—"at present at least."

COMMENT: Although the letter is couched in formal language, the reader cannot fail to detect that Sophia is still very much in love with Tom in spite of his many derelictions. Tom himself is overjoyed and spends, Fielding tells us, three hours "in reading and kissing" the letter.

Next Tom, Partridge, Mrs. Miller and her younger daughter decide to go to a playhouse. The play turns out to be Shakespeare's *Hamlet,* as adapted by Garrick and with Garrick in the leading role. At the conclusion of the play, Tom is approached by a lady whom he recognizes as Mrs. Fitzpatrick. She asks him to visit her, telling him that she has something of consequence to communicate to him.

COMMENT: Considering Fielding's experience as a playwright and manager of a theatre, it was almost inevitable that a playhouse should be the scene of one of his descriptions of London life. That Tom should have gone to see Garrick's *Hamlet* was also predictable: Garrick was the greatest English actor of his time and his *Hamlet* was one of the most talked-about theatrical events of the century.

The fact that the play was *Hamlet* also gave Fielding a chance to exploit for comic effect the simple—mindedness of Partridge. One of

Partridge's characteristics, mentioned again and again in the novel, is a fear of ghosts. Unable to distinguish between art and life, between fiction and reality, Partridge is terrified by the ghost in *Hamlet*.

The reappearance of Harriet Fitzpatrick in the story, with an undisclosed message for Tom, makes the reader curious as to what will happen next and thus ties the playhouse episode into the main plot.

Back in Somersetshire, Blifil has heard from Western that Sophia has been located. He urges Allworthy to accompany him to London, but Allworthy is reluctant since he realizes that Sophia ran away from home to escape the unwelcome attentions of his nephew, and he is opposed to forced matches. Blifil, however, by an histrionic exhibition of the passion he has for Sophia, persuades him at least to give him an opportunity of once more asking for Sophia's hand. Allworthy and Blifil arrive in London on the evening Tom goes to the playhouse.

On the next morning Western and Blifil visit Mrs. Western's lodgings and hurry in "with less ceremony than the laws of visiting require." Sophia turns pale at the sight of Blifil; her aunt lectures the Squire on his lack of courtesy and, professedly, because of the effect of such discourtesy on the tender sensibilities of a delicate girl like Sophia, allows her niece to withdraw to her own room. Western is astonished. He has had reason to think that his sister is in full agreement with him on the desirability of a match with Blifil, and cannot imagine why she should now delay proceedings. Blifill, "who saw a little deeper into things," suspects that there are reasons for Mrs. Western's conduct.

Blifil had reason to be suspicious, for Mrs. Western had indeed altered her plans for Sophia. Lord Fellamar had discovered that he was genuinely in love with Sophia. In the heat of his resentment, he had actually sent his friend, Captain Egglane, to ask Western's permission to seek his daughter's hand in marriage, and had commissioned him, should the request be refused, to issue a challenge. However, when he realized how much he loved Sophia, he wished to rescind his orders, but found out that it was too late.

He then visited Lady Bellaston and told her of his love for Sophia. She encourages him, but warns him that he has a strong rival in Tom Jones. She suggests that he rid himself of this rival by having him seized by a press-gang and sent to sea.

Subsequently Lady Bellaston learns that Mrs. Western has taken lodgings in town. She pays a call on her and acquaints her with the fact that Lord Fellamar is in love with her niece. This seems to Mrs. Western an even better match than that with Blifil, and she agrees to cooperate with Lady Bellaston in bringing it about. The two women then discuss Tom as an obstacle to their plans, and Lady Bellaston maliciously reveals that Tom has had the audacity to address a proposal of marriage to her, and she gives Mrs. Western the letter to use when an opportunity should offer itself. It was shortly after this visit from Lady Bellaston, when Mrs. Western was lecturing her niece on "the folly of love and the wisdom of legal prostitution for hire," that Blifil and Western broke in on the ladies.

We now return to Harriet Fitzpatrick. Before meeting Tom at the theatre, she had called upon Squire Western, who had brutally dismissed her; and she had then called upon Mrs. Western, where she received no kinder reception. She concluded that she had no hopes of gaining a reconciliation with her wealthy uncle and aunt, and she therefore thirsted for revenge. When she saw Tom at the playhouse an idea occurred to her.

Tom, in response to her invitation, visited her in her lodgings. She told him about Fitzpatrick's first paying court to Mrs. Western before turning his attentions to herself, and suggested that Tom might gain access to Sophia by pretending to woo her aunt. Tom politely declines in spite of Harriet's eloquent arguments. He also chooses to ignore Harriet's ill-concealed insinuations that she would not be averse to Tom's romantic attentions.

Meanwhile Fitzpatrick, having been given in Somersetshire Harriet's letter to Mrs. Western, and thereby learning where his wife was now residing, went up to London and was approaching his wife's lodgings just as Tom was coming out. Suspicious as always, he draws his sword and forces Tom into a duel. Tom is obliged to defend himself and in so doing sheathes "one half of his sword in the body" of Fitzpatrick, who drops his sword and cries out: "I am a dead man."

At this moment the press-gang, set upon Tom by Lord Fellamar, arrives at the scene and, believing also that Tom has killed his adversary, decides that there is no point in abducting him now for he is destined "for another port." The officer in charge of the gang, therefore, hales Tom before a magistrate, and he is committed to prison.

His woes multiply. On the next morning, Partridge, in terror lest he encounter the ghost of Fitzpatrick, who, he has heard, was dead, visits Tom and brings him a letter from Sophia, announcing that she has seen his proposal of marriage to Lady Bellaston and desiring that his name "be never more mentioned" to her.

> **COMMENT:** The foregoing section is a remarkable study of the operations of malice. Lady Bellaston, spurned by Tom, is demonic in her desire for revenge. She is prepared to do anything to make

certain that he will not marry Sophia. Harriet Fitzpatrick, on the other hand, is willing to help Tom—chiefly because she knows that the marriage of Tom and Sophia will enrage her uncle and aunt whom she now implacably hates.

BOOK XVII

CONTAINING THREE DAYS

Tom seems to be in dire straits, and in the first chapter of this book Fielding pretends that he is not altogether sure that he can extricate him from his difficulties, for, of course, as an enlightened modern writer, he cannot have recourse to supernatural machinery. With affected solemnity he proclaims: "To natural means alone we are confined." How can he possibly rescue Tom? Perhaps the reader had best prepare to attend the "hero's" hanging.

While Allworthy and Mrs. Miller are breakfasting together, Blifil brings in the news of Tom's duel and imprisonment, and says that he is afraid that this information will shock the Squire "with the remembrance of ever having shown any kindness to such a villain." Mrs. Miller promptly rallies to Tom's defence. Allworthy is surprised, for he has not known that Mrs. Miller knew Tom. Mrs. Miller proceeds to tell Allworthy of Tom's great generosity and kindness, and she expresses disbelief in Blifil's story. When the truth of the story is established, she expresses her certainty that further inquiries will reveal that Tom was innocent of any wrong-doing.

The conversation is interrupted by a violent knocking at the door. Mrs. Miller and her daughter, who has been greatly affected by the terrible news concerning Tom, leave the room and Squire Western bursts in. He is, as usual, voluble, profane, and utterly incoherent, but Allworthy finally understands that Mrs. Western has entered into a conspiracy to marry Sophia off "to a son of a whore of a lord," and that Western is demanding his cooperation in having the marriage of Sophia and Blifil celebrated at once. Allworthy, opposed to forced marriages, demurs. Blifil tells Western that Tom has killed a man and is likely to be hanged, and Western, enraptured at the prospect of the speedy removal of what he conceives to be the chief obstacle to his plans, falls "a-singing and capering about the room." When he departs, Allworthy attempts to persuade Blifil that he will never overcome Sophia's aversion to him, but Blifil's greedy little heart remains set on the financially attractive marriage.

COMMENT: The jaunty tone of the novel as a whole, and especially the jauntiness of the introductory chapters, precludes our taking Tom's "tragic" predicaments seriously. Fielding's manner is that of an entertainer who says, comically and without any conceit or egotism, "Here, look at what tricks I can perform."

The plot of *Tom Jones* is known for its tightness, for the way in which the various parts of the story are deftly stitched together. It may be questioned, however, if this is so much a plot as it is a kind of parody on plots. In other words, the mock-heroic element in this work is all-pervasive and is not confined to those passages in which Fielding amuses himself with the stilted and elevated diction that had come to be associated with the epic style.

Allworthy's enlightened opinions on marriage, as expressed in his long conversation with Western, had more relevance to Fielding's original readers than they have today when practically everybody takes for granted the right of freedom of choice. That right was by no means universally acknowledged in the eighteenth century. Marriages were often arranged and the motives were often avarice or social ambition. Although it would be rash to identify all of Allworthy's pronouncements with Fielding's own opinions, it seems clear that in this passage Allworthy is spokesman for the author.

In the meantime Mrs. Western is doing everything in her power to persuade Sophia of the advantageousness of a marriage with Lord Fellamar. Sophia, however, astonishes (or seems to astonish) her aunt by telling her of Fellamar's outrageous conduct towards her, of the liberties that he had taken with her person and of the further liberties that she suspected, quite properly, that he had in mind. The conversation is interrupted by a visit by Lord Fellamar, which turns out to be a most tedious visit because, after what she has heard of his behavior, Mrs. Western insists on staying in the room.

COMMENT: There is an instructive contrast between Mrs. Western's worship of rank and belief in the supreme importance of a title of nobility, and her brother's utter contempt for the niceties of social position. The eighteenth century was, on the whole, a long way off from the egalitarianism that marks our modern democratic society, but even in the class-conscious and traditionally hierarchic eighteenth century there were not a few people who looked with cynical eyes on the subtleties of distinctions in rank. Property Squire Western understands. Reasons why he should be impressed by a fop like Fellamar he does not understand.

Sophia's revelation to her aunt of Fellamar's familiarities shocks the affected moral sensibilities of that vain and calculating woman, but not so much so that she is persuaded to alter her plans. She stays in the same room with Sophia and Fellamar to protect her niece, but a more compelling reason is her strategic decision that "a little distant behaviour might not be improper to so forward a lover." She is, in other words, tantalizing him and egging him on.

Now Mrs. Miller sallies forth to acquaint Nightingale with the news of Tom's misfortune, only to discover from her grieving daughter that Partridge had already told her husband and Jack had gone to visit Tom. Mrs. Miller thereupon goes to the prison, and she and Nightingale attempt to cheer up the disconsolate Jones. Partridge comes in with the report that Fitzpatrick is still alive, but Tom remains extremely depressed because he, whatever the consequences, thinks the shedding of the blood of one's fellow-creatures a dreadful thing. He is also depressed because of Sophia's last letter. Mrs. Miller agrees to carry a letter from Tom to Sophia.

Mrs. Miller meets with a very civil welcome even though Sophia does not know her. But when she reveals the purpose of her call, Sophia refuses to accept the letter. Mrs. Miller, however, throws herself on her knees and begs for Sophia's compassion, telling her of Tom's extraordinary kindness toward the Andersons and toward her own daughter, Nancy. Sophia at length allows Mrs. Miller to leave the letter with her but does not promise to read it. When Mrs. Miller leaves, she does read it, but finds it a strange letter. It consisted of little more than Tom's "confessions of his own unworthiness, and bitter lamentations of despair, together with the most solemn protestations of his unalterable fidelity to Sophia . . ." Sophia read the letter through twice "with great attention," but Tom's meaning "still remained a riddle to her." She was still angry with him, but her resentment towards Lady Bellaston was so great that she had precious little left over for anyone else.

That afternoon, she, Mrs. Western, and Lady Bellaston were engaged to attend the opera, and to go thence to a "drum." Sophia had no liking for these engagements, but she felt obliged to live up to her commitments, kept her appointments and suffered. Lady Bellaston was especially cruel to her, taking every opportunity "civilly and slily to insult her." The presence of Lord Fellamar, whom they met at the opera, as also oppressive. The dreadful night, however, finally came to an end.

COMMENT: In contrast to the circumstantial account of the visit to the playhouse, the description of the afternoon at the opera is disappointing. The fact of the attendance at the opera, however, reminds us of the growing popularity of opera in England in the eighteenth century.

Fielding himself tells us precisely what an eighteenth-century "drum" was. "A drum, then, is an assembly of well-dressed persons of both sexes, most of whom play at cards, and the rest do nothing at all . . ."

Mrs. Miller eloquently champions Tom's cause to Squire Allworthy, giving him many instances of Tom's goodness and hinting that Blifil may not be as virtuous as he appears to be. Allworthy obviously tries to be just, but feels that Tom deserves the displeasure he has visited upon him, and he expresses resentment of the slurs cast at his nephew.

In the course of this conversation, while Mrs. Miller is arguing the exceptional kindness of Tom, she tells Allworthy how Tom had helped her daughter and Nightingale (without, of course, mentioning the embarrassing fact of Nancy's premature pregnancy), and of Nightingale's father's alienation from his son. Allworthy says that he knows the elder Nightingale and will try to bring him to reason.

Blifil now enters, with Dowling the attorney, who has become a "great favourite with Mr. Blifil" and who has become Allworthy's steward and who hopes to be retained in a similar capacity by Western.

Encouraged by Lady Bellaston and Mrs. Western, Lord Fellamar's courtship of Sophia becomes more ardent, while her resistance is firmer. One day, while he is protesting his love to Sophia and she is exhibiting her repugnance, her aunt bursts into the room, obviously angry, and apologizes for the conduct of Sophia, assuring his lordship that the Western family is conscious of the honor conferred upon them all by his attention. Sophia is distraught by her aunt's action and soon leaves the room "with more appearance of passion than she had ever shown on any occasion." But in her absence Mrs. Western reassures Fellamar that all will soon be well.

Fielding now tells us why Mrs. Western had come into the room so angrily. Sophia's new maid, Betty, had been bribed by Lady Bellaston, through Honour, to report her every action, and it had thus been learned that Sophia had received a letter from Mrs. Miller.

Returning to see if Tom's letter had had any effect, Mrs. Miller was ushered, by previously issued commands, into the presence of Mrs. Western, who interrogated her about the letter. Since Mrs. Miller knew virtually nothing about the contents of the letter, Mrs. Western got little for her pains, but she angrily dismissed Mrs. Miller with gross insults. She then hurried to make further inquiries of Sophia, and thus burst into the room while Lord Fellamar was urging his suit.

After Fellamar's departure, Mrs. Western bitterly upbraided her niece and demanded to see Tom's letter. Sophia pleads the innocence of her conduct and insists that she does not have the letter with her—which is, in a way, the truth. Pressed as to whether or not she will be sensible and marry Fellamar, Sophia gives an emphatic answer, an emphatic negative answer. In her fury, Mrs. Western threatens that she will now return Sophia to the tender mercies of her father.

The scene again shifts and we are back in Tom's prison. Nightingale, who has been searching for witnesses to bolster Tom's defense, mournfully reports that the witnesses he has found give a completely different account of the duel from that given by Tom, even though they had been urged to consider that a man's life was at stake.

While Tom is ruefully attending to the significance of Nightingale's report, Mrs. Miller arrives with more bad news, the news of her latest reception at the lodgings of Mrs. Western.

Tom is now in a state of utter despair, and is not even sure that he wants to live. At this point, the turnkey (jailer) enters and announces that a lady wishes to speak with him. Nightingale and Mrs. Miller leave —and Mrs. Waters enters.

When we last saw Mrs. Waters, she was in a coach with Fitzpatrick and Maclachlan and travelling to Bath. She and Fitzpatrick became attracted to one another and they settled down in Bath as man and wife. And as man and wife they had recently come up to town.

> **COMMENT:** Fielding himself provides the best comment on this stage of the story. He writes: "Whether Mr. Fitzpatrick was so wise a man as not to part with one good thing till he had secured another, which he had at present only a prospect of regaining; or whether Mrs. Waters had so well discharged her office (that of wife), that he intended to retain her as principal, and to make his wife (as is often the case) only her deputy, I will not say; but certain it is, he never mentioned his wife to her, never communicated to her the letter given him by Mrs. Western, nor ever once hinted his intention of repossessing his wife. Much less did he ever mention the name of Jones . . ."

Having at long last discovered that her husband's adversary in the duel was her old friend who had made memorable her stay at the inn at Upton, she has now come to cheer him up. She enters his place of confinement full of gaiety, which contrasts remarkably with Tom's gloom. She proceeds to assure Tom that he has nothing to worry about: Fitzpatrick is not likely to die, and has had the grace to acknowledge before witnesses that he was the aggressor. In his relief, Tom makes solemn promises of amendment. From this moment on he is determined to live a completely virtuous life—much to the astonishment and disappointment of Mrs. Waters, who clearly had other plans in mind.

One of Tom's problems has been, it would seem, solved. He still had to face up to Sophia's intransigence.

BOOK XVIII

THE END

The first chapter is entitled "A Farewell to the Reader." Fielding, spoofingly as usual, says now we must get down to business. No more nonsense! Now we have to resort to "plain narrative" and wind the story up.

Partridge has seen Mrs. Waters leave Tom and has recognized her as Jenny Jones, his former servant and the confessed mother of Tom. In horror he reveals to Tom that Tom has been guilty of incest. A very cryptic letter that soon arrives from Mrs. Waters, mentioning a matter of high importance, gives at least the appearance of support of Partridge's claim.

Black George now arrives to report that Sophia has been returned to her father's residence but is allowed considerable liberty because: a) she has spiritedly refused to marry Fellamar, whom Western despises, and b) because he is certain that Tom is going to be hanged and will therefore be out of the way of Blifil.

Now we turn to Allworthy and to his efforts on behalf of Mrs. Miller's daughter and son-in-law. He visits his old acquaintance, the elder Nightingale, and persuades him to see his son. He then asks about Black George, whom he has seen at Nightingale's house, and learns that George has asked Nightingale to invest some money that he has, in some totally mysterious manner, been able to acquire. The money, on examination, proves to be the money that Allworthy had given Tom when he sorrowfully dismissed him from his household. The Squire asks Nightingale to be quiet for the time being about this affair.

Returning to Mrs. Miller's, Allworthy expressed his confidence that the Nightingales will be reconciled, and he also tells her that he has acquired information advantageous to one of her dear friends—meaning, of course, Tom Jones. In his conversation with Mrs. Miller it is apparent that he is willing to revise his estimate of Tom. For one thing, he has been impressed by what Mrs. Miller herself has told him; for another, he is now impressed by all that young Nightingale, who comes in to thank him for his intervention, tells him about Tom. And he has been conditioned for a change of attitude by a letter he has recently received from Square.

Square, who has been at Bath for his health, has been informed by his doctors that his case is hopeless. He is a doomed man. In this situation, he tries to make restitution for the wrongs that he has done, and he writes Allworthy a sober, factual account of what actually happened on the occasion of Allworthy's supposedly fatal illness. He testifies that Tom has "the noblest generosity of heart, the most perfect capacity for friendship, the highest integrity, and indeed every virtue which can ennoble a man."

In the same post (by a curious coincidence in a novel notorious for its coincidences) there is a letter from Square's old rival, Thwackum, as arrogant and self-righteous as ever, who professes himself not at all surprised to hear a fresh instance of the villainy of the pupil of Square the atheist.

> **COMMENT:** Early in the novel there seemed little to choose between Thwackum, the savage and vindictive clergyman, and Square, the self-satisfied "philosopher." As Square draws near to his death-bed, however, he repents his follies and misdeeds, and we are moved to forgive him. Thwackum remains as odious as ever, and Fielding even tells us that Allworthy himself has never liked Thwackum but did respect his scholarship.
>
> It would be wrong to use the evidence of the two letters to argue that Fielding was a foe of organized religion. It is, on the other hand, proper to observe that Fielding was very conscious of the abuses of religion and of the fact that churchmen are, by virtue of their station and office, in a position to do a great deal of harm.

Nightingale also reveals the results of his inquiry into the testimony against Tom, and in this account says that he saw two members of the press-gang closeted with Mr. Dowling, the lawyer, sent by Allworthy to look after Tom's interests. Allworthy is amazed, for he had not dispatched Dowling on this errand. Blifil enters, and an aroused Allworthy asks him if he had sent the lawyer. Visibly distressed by the question, Blifil acknowledges that he had—but goes on to explain that he had acted out of compassionate motives, hoping that the lawyer could persuade the witnesses to "soften their evidence." Allworthy is satisfied with this explanation, but Mrs. Miller retains her doubts concerning the character of Blifil.

Partridge is summoned, whom Allworthy has not seen for twenty years. He is interrogated by the Squire, who cannot imagine why Partridge persists in denying that he is actually Tom's father when the case against him is so plain. Partridge vehemently repeats his denial and adds that he wishes Allworthy were as wrong in his identification of Tom's mother as of that of his father. No sooner has he horrified Allworthy with the story of Tom's relations with Mrs. Waters, "his mother," than Mrs. Waters herself comes "hastily and abruptly into the room." She greets him courteously and asks to be allowed to speak with him privately.

First, she assured Allworthy that Partridge was telling the truth when he claimed not to be Tom's father. The father, it seems, was a neighbor of Allworthy's, a handsome young man named Summer, son of a clergyman and the recipient of many favors from Allworthy. He had even, after completing his studies at the university, where he had been supported by Allworthy, come to live in Allworthy's house. He had scarcely been one of the household for a year when he was carried off by the smallpox. He then, Allworthy asks in effect, was the father of your child? No, sir, Mrs. Waters replies, but he was the father of Tom Jones. She goes on to startle Allworthy with the almost incredible news that the mother was none other than his sister, Bridget, who, after taking every precaution to insure secrecy, had engaged Jenny Jones and Jenny's mother to attend her at the birth of the infant. The Squire is dumbfounded but Mrs. Waters' narration is too circumstantial to be doubted. He expresses considerable resentment of his sister's conduct in carrying her secret to the grave, but Mrs. Waters says that she had every intention of confessing the truth to her brother and had delayed because Allworthy had seemed to take such a liking to the boy. She adds that she feels strongly for all of Tom's misfortunes and is especially surprised that Allworthy should have employed his own lawyer "to prosecute him for a murder of which he was not guilty."

Allworthy protests that she has been misinformed, whereupon she explains that Dowling had actually come to her, thinking that she was Fitzpatrick's wife, and had told her that she would be assisted with any money she wanted to carry on the prosecution, and that the money would be provided by a very worthy gentleman who knew what a villain Jones was. Since she discovered that Dowling (who had refused to give her his name but had been recognized by Partridge, who had known him years before) was Allworthy's steward, she assumed that "the worthy gentleman" was Allworthy.

Squire Western breaks in upon this conversation, ranting in his usual way about the trouble he is having with his daughter. He has discovered that Sophia had received a letter from Tom, and, worse still, that Tom is about to be released from prison. He demands that Allworthy join with him in bringing about the marriage of Sophia and Blifil, threatening that if she does not yield to his wishes he will lock her in a garret for the rest of her days and keep her on nothing but bread and water.

Allworthy finds out that Western has heard of Tom's forthcoming release from Dowling. He learns that Dowling and a few other lawyers are meeting soon at Western's lodgings to settle a matter involving a mortgage, a matter in which the elder Nightingale is interested.

When Western leaves, Allworthy resumes his conversation with Mrs. Waters and expresses his disappointment at the kind of life she has led.

She thereupon gives him a detailed account of all that has happened to her since she left Allworthy's neighborhood. She was first "betrayed by the most solemn promises of marriage," and had been forced, as it were, to make the best of things; and she maintained that she was at least faithful to her betrayer and felt that, in the "eye of Heaven," she was really married. Afer the death of this first lover, with her reputation gone, she could hardly expect an honorable proposal of marriage. "Necessity" drove her into the arms of Captain Waters, who had, just before her meeting with Tom, marched away to fight the Jacobite rebels.

> **COMMENT:** It is clear now that the story is hurrying to its end. The secret of Tom's birth has been revealed—and much of the conduct of Bridget toward the foundling explained. That Allworthy should have been deceived by a man he had done much for, indeed had practically adopted, and by his sanctimonious sister, was almost inevitable in view of Fielding's remorselessly ironic view of life.
>
> Mrs. Waters' narrative is of primary importance because of this revelation, but it is also important for its relevance to Fielding's views on marriage. Betrayed innocence is no longer a theme that a novelist is likely to use; even in the eighteenth century it was a rather tired theme, but the greater stratification of society in that century made it more plausible than it has since become.
>
> Fielding uses the theme not for its sentimental value—Mrs. Waters is scarcely the conventional betrayed heroine—but because it enables him to ask important questions about the true nature of marriage. Is it merely a ceremony?

Now Dowling comes into the room. On seeing Mrs. Waters he tries to withdraw, but is too late. Allworthy bolts the door of the room and subjects Dowling to a grueling cross-examination. Dowling acknowledges that Blifil had sent him to Fitzpatrick's wife—he had understandably confused her with Mrs. Waters—and to the two sailors who were witnesses of the duel. He professes to have believed that Blifil was acting in accordance with his uncle's instructions. "You would not have thought, I believe," says Allworthy, "to have obliged me, had you known that this Mr. Jones was my own nephew." Dowling hastens to assure him that he had known this, that Mrs. Blifil had told him the facts about Tom when she commissioned him to deliver a letter to Allworthy written just before her death. Allworthy protests that he had never received this letter, and learns that it had been delivered into the hands of Blifil. Assured by Blifil that the secret of Tom's birth had been communicated to Allworthy, Dowling could only assume that Allworthy intended to preserve the secret.

Allworthy orders Dowling to keep their conversation in the strictest confidence. He proceeds, however, to explain to Mrs. Miller that Tom is his sister's son and that he has learned that he is also "the brother of that wicked viper which I have so long nurtured in my bosom." Mrs. Waters and Mrs. Miller are overjoyed at the way things are going. Allworthy has a chair (sedan chair) summoned and departs, but not before Blifil, hearing the call for the chair, obsequiously attends upon his uncle and sneakily tries to find out where he is going. Just before he departs, the grim Allworthy turns on his nephew, whose villainy has now been unmasked, and says, "Harkee, sir, do you find out, before my return, the letter which your mother sent me on her death-bed?"

Allworthy is carried to Western's lodgings and apologizes for the disagreeable proposals made by the odious Blifil. He also sings the praises of his nephew Tom. Western, coming in and being acquainted with the fact of Tom's restoration to favor, joins Allworthy in the commendation of Tom, whom he had always liked but whom he had opposed for purely avaricious reasons. Sophia, however, is as vehement in her rejection of Tom as she had been in her rejection of Blifil.

> **COMMENT:** Fielding seems to be teasing his readers as he spins out the ending of his story. It is obvious (and always has been) that there is going to be a happy ending. Tom's identity has been established. Blifil's villainy has been exposed. Tom and Allworthy have been reconciled. Western espouses Tom's cause. But Sophia—and with some reason—remains adamant.

When Tom is released from prison, there is a touching scene when he waits upon his benevolent uncle. They discourse on the nature of virtue, and Tom expresses sorrow for all of his past offenses. He confides in his uncle that he is particularly sad because he has lost "a treasure." Allworthy is sympathetic, knowing, of course, that he is referring to Sophia, but urges Tom not to be too importunate in his suit.

Western is announced, and Allworthy goes down to meet him. Then Mrs. Miller arrives, who has again visited Sophia on Tom's behalf but has found her inexorable. She does not, however, think that Tom should despair, for she told Sophia of Tom's forthright rejection of Arabella Hunt's proposal (Book XV, Chapter XI), and Sophia blushed and stammered, "I will not deny but that I believe he has some affection for me."

While Tom is reflecting on what Mrs. Miller has told him, Western, now impatient to have him for a son-in-law, forces his way into the room in spite of the remonstrances of Allworthy, proclaims his affection for Tom, and tries to carry him off to Sophia. Both Tom and his uncle urge moderation but agree to join Western for tea, on which occasion Sophia will undoubtedly be present.

Fielding now tells us some of the details of Tom's release from prison. The lieutenant, in charge of the press-gang employed by Lord Fellamar to abduct Tom, was very impressed by Tom's obvious gentlemanliness, and assured Fellamar that he must have been mistaken in his opinion of the character of Tom. A little later, Fellamar dined with an Irish peer and heard that Fitzpatrick was a scoundrel, and that he intended to persuade him to consent to a separation from his wife.

Fitzpatrick no longer seems terribly interested in the wife he had so violently pursued in Upton, and is willing to acknowledge both the innocence and the merits of Tom.

> **COMMENT:** Fielding is being deliberately cryptic. Who is the Irish peer? Can there be any doubt that he is the Irish peer who has been carrying on with Harriet?

"And now a message was brought from Mr. Blifil, desiring to know if his uncle was at leisure. . . . Allworthy started and turned pale, and then in a more passionate tone than I believe he had ever used before, bid the servant tell Blifil he knew him not." Tom, despite all that Blifil has done to him, shows the nobility of his spirit by interceding for his half-brother. Mrs. Miller comes in and she too is unhappy about having Blifil in her house. Tom's forbearance seems to her almost beyond belief, but it is nonetheless genuine. Tom actually goes to Blifil's room, offers him forgiveness and money, but urges upon him the necessity of his quitting the Miller house.

Tom returns to Allworthy and next learns of Black George's wickedness in retaining the money given Tom by Allworthy which he had lost on his first setting out from Allworthy's home (Book VI, Chapter XII). Tom is at first "shocked beyond measure," but soon concludes that there had been no malice in George's act, that his situation made the temptation too great, and that, all in all, George was his friend. The benevolent Allworthy cannot share the lenient attitude of Tom, and expresses his determination to punish George as much as the law makes possible.

Now Tom, joined by his friend and voluntary servant, the whimsical and ludicrous Partridge, dresses for the tea with Sophia and her father. When they arrive at the Western's, it is apparent that Sophia has taken pains with her preparations. Squire Western soon discovers that he has private business with Allworthy, and Tom and Sophia are left alone. Sophia politely congratulates Tom on his good fortune, only to be told that his happiness is far from complete. She and Tom debate the place of justice and mercy in human judgments, and Tom gradually prevails over an imperfectly reluctant Sophia. They embrace passionately.

Western, who has been eagerly listening to the conversation from behind a closed door, rushes into the room and demands to know when the wedding is to take place. Sophia affects to be opposed to precipitate action, but when her father charges her again with willfulness, she decides to become a most dutiful daughter and agrees to marry Tom on the following day.

COMMENT: If there is a hyperbolic quality to the goodness of Tom in the closing pages of this novel, it is designed to balance the author's preoccupation with Tom's several lapses from virtue. It is also, of course, part of Fielding's ironic awareness of the distance of art from life; it is part of his mock-heroic manner; it is a satiric thrust at eighteenth-century sentimentalism.

Although the story actually comes to an end when Sophia marries Tom, the reader, according to the conventions of story-telling accepted by Fielding, is entitled to know what happened to the other central characters.

1) Allworthy steadfastly refused to see Blifil, but was persuaded by Tom and Sophia to settle a generous annuity on him. When we leave Blifil he has turned Methodist and is hoping to marry a rich widow of that religious sect. Fielding's attitude toward Methodism is unquestionably spiteful and unfair, but is far from an uncommon attitude, especially for those of Fielding's class. And in fairness to Fielding, it should be observed that he is no more virulent on the subject of Methodism than he is onother religious subjects. Catholics do not fare well. Quakers do not fare well. Even representatives of the Established Church are held up to ridicule.

   It must be emphasized, however, that Fielding is not against religion; he is only against abuses. Whatever toes he may have trod on, he was always fighting on the side of the angels.

2) Square, after writing his repentant letter to Allworthy, died. Thwackum, having by his letter completely alienated the affection (such as it was) of Allworthy, was, as the story concludes, still trying to worm his way back into the Squire's good graces—with little hope of success.

3) Mrs. Fitzpatrick, Fielding tells us with beautifully controlled irony, lives in a fashionable part of London, separated from her husband, with a very small fortune, but she is "so good an economist" that she can spend three times her income. She is also, says Fielding drily, a great friend of the Irish peer's wife.

4) "Mrs. Western was soon reconciled to her niece Sophia, and hath spent two months together with her in the country. Lady Bellaston made the latter a formal visit at her return to town, where she behaved to Jones as to a perfect stranger, and, with great civility, wished him joy on his marriage."

5) The elder Nightingale purchased a country seat for his son and daughter-in-law in the neighborhood where Tom and Sophia have settled. Mrs. Miller and her younger daughter have taken up residence with the Nightingales.

6) Surprisingly (but deliberately surprisingly), Mrs. Waters has married Parson Supple. Allworthy has settled a generous annual sum on her, and Sophia has persuaded her father to procure for Supple an advantageous church living.

7) Black George has run away and never been heard of again. (We recall Allworthy's determination to prosecute him for the misappropriation of Tom's money.) Tom gives money to the Seagrim family, "but not in equal proportions, for Molly had much the greatest share."

8) Tom establishes a generous annuity for Partridge, who again opens a school, this time with better hopes of success, and who hopes to marry Molly.

9) Tom and Sophia have taken over Western's home, Western having removed to another part of the country where he thinks the hunting is superior. But the ranting Squire dotes on his two grandchildren, and Allworthy gives continuing evidence of his deep affection for his nephew and Sophia.

A "history," the novel ends like a romance—but this is surely part of Fielding's joke, part of his satire, part of his parody. It is also expressive of the unconquerable optimism, underlying the cynicism and disenchantment with man and his ways, that informs so much of the story.

THE CENTRAL CHARACTERS: AN ANALYSIS

TOM JONES: In some respects, Fielding's hero represents a protest against the very notion of a hero. Richardson's heroines, Pamela and Clarissa, epitomized virtue, and by the very fact of their function as symbols seemed to Fielding to be far removed from life. Tom's badness is not designed to titillate; it is, rather, a dramatization of one of Fielding's deepest convictions: given fallen human nature, there is no such thing as absolute goodness; all of us are strange mixtures of good and bad; virtue is not inbred in us but is achieved after a long and painful struggle with our rebellious senses and chaotic instincts.

If, on the one hand, however, Tom was created to refute the burgeoning sentimentalism of the eighteenth century, he also curiously partakes of that sentimentalism. He is, in other words, an anti-hero; but Fielding also feels that he must make it plain to his readers that he takes Tom seriously, and so Tom must be simultaneously a hero, a recognizable, a conventional hero. One of the most interesting features of this novel is the conflict between realism and romanticism, between the relentless exhibition of Tom in all of his weaknesses, and of Tom as an embodiment of the author's ideal.

BLIFIL: The character of Tom Jones and Fielding's message cannot be completely understood without Blifil. The virtues of Tom acquire special significance when they are seen in violent contrast with the detestable vices of Blifil. It may be urged that Blifil's villainy is so complete as to be unbelievable; to this charge the only answer is that Fielding was not writing for a public that needed or demanded realism. Fielding served his literary apprenticeship in the theatre. He knew that audiences loved to hiss the villain. So it is with Blifil. We all hate and despise him—but through the magic of art we *love* to hate and despise him. The situation is not unlike that in Shakespeare's *Othello*. There is no question but what Iago is shockingly evil, but he remains one of the most perpetually interesting characters in literature.

Blifil, of course, does not exist solely to illuminate the character of Tom. He also serves Fielding's purpose as an embodiment of the hypocrisy and false values of the age. And, paradoxically, he contributes to the fun of this bouncy and exuberant novel.

ALLWORTHY: In Fielding's rather unsystematic view of ethics, virtue and benevolence (good will, charity) go hand in hand as, indeed, they do in most meaningful ethical codes. Allworthy is explicitly set forth as the good and benevolent man. But Fielding cannot repress his irony: Allworthy, the totally virtuous man, is, in a manner of speaking, the victim of his own virtue. He is so concerned with justice that he makes hideous mistakes. He is deceived by his sister, by young Blifil, by Dowling. He demonstrates his benevolence by his treatment of Thwackum and Square, though neither have any just claim to it. He is a conscientious magistrate, but is far from infallible. He accepts the confession of Jenny Jones—without corroboration. He finds Partridge the schoolmaster guilty—without sufficient proof.

SOPHIA WESTERN: In some respects a conventional heroine, young, beautiful, gracious, and virtuous, Sophia also has individuality. She is a dutiful daughter but she has strong feelings concerning the limits of parental authority. It should also be pointed out that her virtue is far removed from priggishness. However much she may have been hurt and affronted by Tom's misadventures, she finds it in her heart to forgive him, not once but many times, and she finally consents to become his wife. In a sense her virtue is not only her own but also stands for that virtue towards which Tom is striving.

SQUIRE WESTERN: Fielding does many things with Western. He uses him as a means of satirizing ignorant countrymen, men of property but of no refinement. Western knows horses and dogs, loves country pleasures like fox-hunting, but is utterly contemptuous of civilized values. Fielding also makes Western a type of cruel parent. He thinks that he loves his daughter but he is determined that she will make an advantageous match even if the prospective husband is utterly detestable to her. Fielding furthermore gets variety into his narrative style by having Western speak in a broad and comic Somersetshire dialect.

MRS. WESTERN: Alternately siding with and quarreling with her brother, Mrs. Western is, like the Squire, both a comic and a villainous creature. In her airy assurance that she knows all about fashionable London life while her brother is brutish and ignorant, she is amusing. In her determination to arrange what she considers a suitable marriage for Sophia, she reveals the corruption of her heart and her total ignorance of essential values.

Mrs. Western's presence in the story also helps Fielding to explain things that might puzzle the reader. For example, how does one account for Sophia's cultivated manners? Brought up by her father on a remote country estate, she is scarcely likely to have been trained to move easily and gracefully in polite society. But she was not brought up by her father; she was educated by her aunt, who, for all of her snobbishness, did move in the fashionable world. And why did Sophia, when she determined to run away from home rather than marry Blifil, decide to go up to London? Because through her aunt she had become acquainted with Lady Bellaston and had reason to believe that Lady Bellaston would befriend her.

The modern reader should, perhaps, be told that the title "Mrs." was used not only for married women but also for unmarried women who had reached a certain age. There is little in the way of precise definition of what the certain age was; in general, when it began to look as if a woman was likely to remain a spinster, the use of the honorific "Mrs." was extended to her.

THE BLIFIL BROTHERS: In Dr. Blifil, Fielding satirizes vain and foolish learning. The doctor "was master of almost every other science but that by which he was to get his bread; the consequence of which was, the doctor at the age of forty had no bread to eat." Allworthy's kindness to Dr. Blifil is evidence of the goodness of his heart, but there is a faint hint in Fielding's account that Allworthy was too easily imposed upon. Dr. Blifil's fortune-hunting instincts, frustrated not because he happened to be married but because Allworthy knew he was, leads him to introduce his younger brother, Captain Blifil, into the Allworthy household—and this self-seeking, avaricious action ironically leads to his death from a broken heart. That Dr. Blifil dies is, as is obvious, a way of getting him out of the story after he has served his usefulness; that he dies of a broken heart is a kind of parody on an overworked literary motif, and as parody fits in with the mock-heroic style of the novel.

Captain Blifil's most important function in the novel is the siring of young Blifil. By his hypocrisy and cant (traits Fielding, rightly or wrongly, was inclined to associate with Methodism), he wins the hand of aging and anxious Bridget. Their son is, significantly, born only eight months after the marriage, rids himself of his brother, with whom he has no intention of sharing the fortune he dreams of coming into, and then, ironically, dies himself before his dreams come true.

BRIDGET ALLWORTHY: At first her smug and self-satisfied religiosity is used to define, by means of contrast, the more genuine goodness of her brother. She also, of course, is a comic old maid, desperately in search of a husband, and thus the predestined dupe of any fortune-hunter. Fielding also hints that, for all of her affected interest in religious discourse, there is no small amount of sensuality in her character—and he thus subtly prepares the reader for the startling revelation that she is the mother of the foundling deposited in Allworthy's bed.

Both Bridget and Captain Blifil marry for the wrong reasons: she merely to escape spinsterhood, he to get a fortune. It is not surprising that they soon come to hate one another. Fielding gives a graphic picture of the horrors of a loveless marriage; since many marriages in the eighteenth century were contracted for practical reasons, this picture serves not only the purposes of the story but also as a commentary on the age.

JENNY JONES (MRS. WATERS): A central figure in the complicated plot of *Tom Jones,* her actions tend to blur rather than to reveal her character. When we first meet her, for example, she is represented as an enterprising and intelligent girl and the innocent victim of envy and malice. A little later it is made clear that the suspicions of the schoolmaster's wife are exposed as baseless. When we next meet her (though as yet we do not know who she is), struggling with Northerton near the residence of the Man of the Hill, she promptly exhibits a kind of shamelessness. She refuses Tom's offer of his coat even though modesty and discretion would seem to have prompted her acceptance, and it is immediately made clear that she is more than willing that Tom should become conscious of her not inconsiderable charms. Her shamelessness increases and leads to Tom's fall from grace in the inn at Upton. We also learn that she is living with a Captain Waters but that there is doubt about the regularity of their union. And we learn that she is involved in an affair with the army officer, Ensign (then a rank in the British army) Northerton. A little later she goes off to Bath with the wild Irishman, Fitzpatrick.

When she re-appears on the scene, however, she comes as Tom's good-hearted supporter and thus enlists our sympathy. Her circumstantial account of her checkered career, given to Allworthy, further stresses her good qualities.

In part, it would seem, she exists to demonstrate one of Fielding's favorite theses, that we are all mixtures of good and bad. In part, too, she exists to provide Fielding with a means of taking his reader by surprise. The blurring of her character comes about because Fielding insists on his right to reticence. He does not feel obliged to tell everything about a character at once. When we get our information piecemeal, especially in a novel as large as this, it is understandably difficult to form a clear idea about a character.

PARTRIDGE: What has been said of Mrs. Waters can also be said of Partridge. When we first encounter him, he is merely a very poor and henpecked schoolmaster and the benefactor of Jenny Jones. Lately he is essentially a comic figure, a barber who makes a great show of learning and who is fond of quoting fragments of Latin. He attaches himself to Tom, accompanies Tom on his travels, and by his obstinate refusal to believe Tom's story of his being disowned by Allworthy, he plays a very important role in the unfolding of the plot.

Partridge is not, however, a simple, good-hearted comical fellow. Fielding is at pains to emphasize his cowardice, his sympathies with the Jacobites and Catholics, and his ludicrous superstitions, particularly his morbid fear of ghosts. He is unreliable and a fool, at times a dangerous fool. He is a useful character in that he is an essential part of the plot and provides Fielding with opportunities to comment on the endless variety of man's follies and vices. But he is a rather strange character, sometimes moving us to laughter, sometimes engaging our affections, and sometimes prompting our scorn. At the very end of the story he seems a most unlikely suitor of wanton Molly Seagrim.

LADY BELLASTON: Through Lady Bellaston, Fielding exposes the false values of the so-called fashionable world. Lascivious and thoroughly vicious, she brings Tom to the lowest point in his moral career. If we see *Tom Jones* as a kind of spiritual pilgrimage (noting, of course, that this way of looking at the novel should be approached with caution or we face the danger of being false to its spirit and tone), she is Tom's last and greatest temptation. When he has finally escaped from this Circe, he is ready for the good and pure love of Sophia.

FITZPATRICK: An Irish fortune-hunter who woos the wealthy Mrs. Western and then transfers his attentions to Harriet, Fitzpatrick provides Fielding with a chance to make many telling observations on marriage, particularly on the abuses of marriage common in his time. Fitzpatrick, especially through his relationship with Mrs. Waters, plays a very important part in the plot.

It is not accidental that Fitzpatrick is represented as an Irishman. Just as many Englishmen shared Dr. Johnson's notorious (and perhaps not altogether serious) antagonism toward Scotsmen, many eighteenth-century Englishmen disliked, or affected to dislike, the Irish. Fitzpatrick conforms to the stereotype: he is "wild," hot-tempered, and opportunistic.

HARRIET FITZPATRICK: Sophia's cousin, Harriet first appeals to our sympathies: she is the abused wife, victim of Fitzpatrick's cruelty and unfaithfulness. Her marriage cost her her fortune, which was quickly dissipated by her husband, and lost her the friendship of Western and his sister. (Mrs. Western was utterly implacable because of the fact that Harriet had, as it were, snatched Fitzpatrick from her own avid grasp.) Later we realize that Harriet is by no means the pathetic creature she represents herself to be. She enjoys the friendship of an "Irish peer," and Fielding more than hints that the friendship goes beyond the Platonic. Harriet is mean, treacherous, and a strikingly effective foil for the virtues of Sophia.

JACK NIGHTINGALE: Tom's friend, an idle trifler, Nightingale is, as it were, redeemed by his marriage to Nancy Miller. The trials and tribulations that he faced before the marriage could form a kind of sub-plot, a story within the main story, related to the main story but interesting in itself.

MRS. MILLER: Widow of a clergyman, Mrs. Miller was under obligations to Squire Allworthy for his generous relief of her distress. Tom, having heard Allworthy speak of her, naturally looks for lodgings in her house when he arrives in London, and thus the stage is set for the reunion with his stepfather. Mrs. Miller's fondness for Tom contributes greatly to Tom's ultimate good fortune.

LORD FELLAMAR: Used primarily by Lady Bellaston as an instrument for her revenge, Fellamar's character is partly defined by his weak compliance with Lady Bellaston's depraved schemes. On the whole a contemptible character, like so many of Fielding's characters he provides moments of comic relief. Of special importance in this regard are the meetings between Fellamar and Western.

THWACKUM: The name is suggestive. Thwackum is immoderately fond of corporal punishment. He is a clergyman—and thinks that virtue can be forced. Although Allworthy had never liked him, he considered him a man of learning and of sound religious principles and had, accordingly, admitted him to his household. Thwackum's last vindictive letter about Tom's villainy, however, alienates Allworthy's sympathies.

SQUARE: Another learned member of Allworthy's menage, Square is constantly at odds with Thwackum. Square represents the new, enlightened, philosophical way of looking at things. He stands for Rationalism, and is fundamentally Deist in his religious thinking (see Chapter I of this book). He seems to have been a follower of the Third Earl of Shaftesbury (1671-1713), one of the most influential of English Deist thinkers. Although Square's philosophy is satirized by Fielding, it is probably because it is philosophy rather than because it is Deist. Fielding was suspicious of abstractions. He felt happier in a world of concrete realities. It is, perhaps, significant that Square, toward the end of his life, asks forgiveness for his past offenses and thus dies in the friendship of Allworthy and Tom.

DOWLING: One scarcely notices the first appearance of Dowling. It comes as a great surprise, then, at the end of the story, when it is revealed that he had all along known the secret of Tom's birth and had kept silent only because he had thought that Allworthy also knew it. He is not, however, entirely the victim of Blifil's dishonesty. He shows himself willing to cooperate in some of Blifil's most diabolic schemes.

BLACK GEORGE SEAGRIM: Allworthy's gamekeeper, his troubles serve to point up Tom's generosity, compassion, and goodness of heart. In spite of all that Tom does for him, when he finds the £500 that Tom loses in first setting out from Allworthy's home, he pockets it, thus making Tom virtually destitute. He is an important part of Fielding's sardonic, ironic view of life.

MOLLY SEAGRIM: Tom's misadventures with Molly are a kind of prologue to his subsequent lapses. Paradoxically, Molly is used to define, as it were, Tom's "innocence." To some extent, of course, Tom was betrayed by his own young passions; he was also, and perhaps more significantly, betrayed by his guilelessness.

MRS. HONOUR: The name, as opposed to Thwackum's, is ironic. Mrs. Honour is completely dishonorable. She is Sophia's maid, and is willing to serve her mistress only insofar as can see advantage to herself. Toward the end of the novel she enters the service of Lady Bellaston. They deserve one another.

DEBORAH WILKINS: One of Allworthy's servants, she represents ludicrous prudishness and savage virtue. She is meddlesome and stupid.

PARSON SUPPLE: Church livings in the eighteenth century were often at the disposal of wealthy landowners, and churchmen were often obliged to be obsequious in their behavior toward their patrons. Supple, a hard-drinking and gluttonous clergyman, is a kind of caricature of the country parson of Fielding's day. He is, it may be said, a stock figure, that is, his characteristics had been exploited by many writers before Fielding, and readers experience the pleasure not of meeting an "original" character but of recognizing a familiar one.

ENSIGN NORTHERTON: He is a very important character in the section of *Tom Jones* given over to Tom's adventures on the road. He is particularly important in that his attempted murder of Mrs. Waters leads to the wildly hectic night at the inn at Upton.

ANDERSON: The pathetic and ineffectual highwayman who is treated generously by Tom, Anderson (though not in his role as highwayman) is a friend of Mrs. Miller. It is largely through Tom's extravagant munificence toward the destitute Anderson family that Mrs. Miller comes to know his essential goodness. Through his actions toward Anderson, Tom demonstrates, even before the final revelations, his true kinship to Allworthy.

ARABELLA HUNT: The somewhat ardent widow who sees Tom at Mrs. Miller's and who goes so far as to send him a proposal of marriage, Arabella Hunt alerts us to Tom's reformation. Through desperate need, Tom succumbed to the lustful demands of Lady Bellaston. Still in need, Tom has now vowed to be worthy of Sophia and rejects Mrs. Hunt's proposal. Of course, the proposal is also comic and part of Fielding's sly commentary on widowhood.

TOM JONES: A CRITICAL APPRAISAL

F. R. Leavis, a pungent, strong-minded, challenging, and controversial critic who has done much, both positively and negatively, to shape our present-day attitudes, once dismissed Fielding as important only insofar as he prepared the way for Jane Austen. One of Fielding's own contemporaries was even more unkind. "Fielding being mentioned," Boswell tells us in his great biography, "Johnson exclaimed, 'he was a blockhead;' and upon my expressing my astonishment at so strange an assertion, he said, 'What I mean by his being a blockhead is that he was a barren rascal.' BOSWELL: 'Will you not allow, Sir, that he draws very natural pictures of human life?' JOHNSON: 'Why, Sir, it is of very low life. Richardson used to say, that had he not known who Fielding was, he should have believed that he was an ostler. Sir, there is more knowledge of the human heart in one letter of Richardson's, than in all "Tom Jones".' "

Both Leavis and Johnson are professed moralists—inevitably very different from one another because conditioned by totally different cultures. One feels that Johnson was displeased with Fielding because of his rowdiness; Leavis, because of a certain slapdash quality of his style, a lack of high seriousness.

Although, of course, there were exceptions, nineteenth-century critics as a whole followed Johnson in his squeamishness and anticipated Leavis in his.

It is now, however, generally taken for granted that Fielding is one of the major English novelists. There is no question but what Cervantes' *Don Quixote* had a great influence on him, and today most readers are prepared to look upon *Tom Jones* as no unworthy successor to that supreme masterpiece of Spanish literature.

Fielding's reputation is now thought to rest on some of the following:

1) His fundamental seriousness. Some of his contemporaries and many of his nineteenth-century readers were misled by his cheerful acceptance of the fact that much in this life is seamy and sordid. Most readers today see that Fielding is actually a passionately moral author. The doctrine of charity is at the core of most significant ethical codes, and Fielding's *Tom Jones* is one of the gayest, most unpretentious, and most eloquent pleas for charity that has ever been written. We are asked to forgive Tom because he has the virtue of charity. At times, he does impetuous things; at times he

yields to his instincts and is false to his ideals; at times he is foolish. But he always has a natively gifted heart. He has natural grace.

Fielding's preoccupation with crucial moral problems can also be seen in his villains. False pride, sanctimoniousness, hypocrisy, selfishness, deceit, malice, envy, vengefulness—these and any number of other vices are excoriated in this superficially light-hearted novel.

2) The brilliance of his style. Fielding was instinctively a gentleman. This means that he detested ostentation (a man who has to *prove* that he is a gentleman is no gentleman), pedantry, dullness. It means that he prized wit, urbanity, easiness. Instinctively a gentleman and actually a gentleman by birth, Fielding, as author, was egalitarian, democratic. He admits all readers into the most intimate companionship with himself.

At the same time, while his tone and spirit are democratic—explicitly anti-aristocratic—his novel is "literary" and sophisticated. The tone, breezy and informal, tends to obscure this. But *Tom Jones* is shot through with allusions—allusions to Pope, to Addison and Steele, to Shaftesbury, to Locke, to classical authors, to French authors—so that one realizes that Fielding's ideal *audience* was one that shared his own interests and education. Putting this another way, Fielding demonstrably wrote for *two* audiences: one, a small and select audience of his peers who could really appreciate his most recondite jokes; another, the reading public as a whole, a public which in his day was growing rapidly but whose relish for graceful allusion and subtle wit was still to be tested.

3) His realism. Few writers have "caught" an age as Fielding has caught his. The sights and sounds of eighteenth-century England are all in this miraculous novel. There is the lovely English countryside, especially the spacious landscape of the West, of Somersetshire, of the nostalgic world of Fielding's own boyhood. There are fox-hunts and all kinds of other country pleasures. There are even illegitimate pleasures such as Tom's youthful dalliance with the more than acquiescent Molly. There is village life, described without a trace of false romanticism. We see sins like envy. We see vulgar brawls such as that stirred up by Molly's indiscreet flaunting of her finery in church.

There is the English eighteenth-century road, with highwaymen, squalid inns, dishonest innkeepers. Fielding set his novel at the time of the outbreak of the Jacobite Rebellion of 1745, and the excitement of that dramatic moment in history is effectively re-created in this novel.

There is, finally, London — to eighteenth-century Englishmen the very heart of the civilized world. The cultural supremacy of France was, in a way, acknowledged, but it was grudgingly acknowledged. France was, on the whole, looked upon as necessary, important — and thoroughly regrettable.

Although aristocratic in his instincts, Fielding was under no illusions about fashionable life. He knew that behind the facade of politeness lurked viciousness and folly. He knew that the possession of a title was no guarantee of either virtue or manners.

4) His audacity. If, on the one hand, Fielding is realistic, on the other he must be looked upon as violently anti-realistic. He plants our feet firmly in what, we think, seems to be Fielding's country and century. And then, mischievously, he reveals that we are not in eighteenth-century England at all: we are in Fielding-land. Fielding-land is a place where the wildest coincidences can take place. It is a land in which everything is a little bit larger than life. Good people are almost unbelievable, like Squire Allworthy. Wicked people are even more unbelievable, like Blifil or Lady Bellaston.

Fieldding's art (and, by extension, his relationship to reality) ought to be compared with the art of that great caricaturist (and serious artist), William Hogarth (1697-1764). Fielding understood the uses of the grotesque. He particularly understood how the grotesque in art could illuminate the actual.

5) His wit and humor. Fielding is among the most cheerful of writers. He also belongs among the most courageous of men because he was never a man favored by fortune. *Tom Jones* is one of the jauntiest of novels, but it was written when Fielding was in ill health, when he was plagued by death, and when his life had been darkened by the death of his wife and daughter.

6) The fertility of his imagination. Although his characters can hardly be said to have been explored in depth, they are rema·kable proof of Fielding's inventiveness, sense of fun, and technical ability in subordinating character to plot. Almost all the major characters are universally recognized as masterpieces. They are all unforgettable. One may at times be disposed to laugh at Squire Western, at times to be disgusted by his brutishness. One is not likely to forget him. Nor can one forget the odious Blifil. It is clear that Blifil is a stage villain—but so is Iago. Fielding is joyously creative and joyously contemptuous of Philistinism.

The new reader of Fielding's greatest novel will be well advised that he ought, first, to enjoy the book. It was written for his enjoyment. It can be enjoyed without much special information.

The reader ought next to realize that he can considerably increase his own enjoyment of this work if he takes the trouble to look into Fielding's life and Fielding's world. A few suggestions as to how to proceed follow in the next chapters.

EXAMINATION QUESTIONS AND ANSWERS

1. Point out some notable instances of Fielding's irony.

ANSWER: When Allworthy in his role as magistrate treats Jenny Jones, the self-confessed mother of the foundling, with kindness and compassion, suspicion quickly settles on the Squire as the infan't father. This is ironically described by Fielding as "the good-natured disposition of the mob." Book I, Chapter IX.

Fielding speaks of those who are dependent on patronage as "less welcome to a great man's table because they stand in need of it." Book I, Chapter X.

On Dr. Blifil's affectation of religion as a way of ingratiating himself with Bridget Allworthy, Fielding remarks: "As sympathies of all kinds are apt to beget love, so experience teaches us that none have a more direct tendency this way then those of a religious kind between persons of different sexes." Book I, Chapter X.

The sanctimoniousness and hypocrisy of Doctor Blifil is effectively exposed in the following passage, which also, incidentally, satirizes the servility of some clergymen: "Here Allworthy concluded his sermon, to which Blifil had listened with the profoundest attention, though it cost him some pains to prevent now and then a small discomposure of his muscles. He now praised every period of what he had heard with the warmth of a young divine, who hath the honour to dine with a bishop the same day in which his lordship hath mounted the pulpit." Book I, Chapter XII.

When Fielding tells us that eight months "after the celebration of the nuptials between Captain Blifil and Miss Bridget Allworthy" a son was born, he ironically explains the premature birth by attributing it to "a fright" experienced by the mother. Book II, Chapter II.

There is irony in Mrs. Partridge's employment of Jenny Jones as servant. Involved is the delusive feeling that men will not be tempted by girls who are plain (Jenny Jones was first described as "no very comely girl"), and a further irony becomes apparent later in the story when the reader learns about the character of "Mrs. Waters." In order to guard herself, we are told, against "matrimonial injuries in her own house," Mrs. Partridge always chose her servants "out of that order of females whose faces are taken as a kind of security for their virtue." Book II, Chapter III.

There is in Chapter IV of the Second Book a magnificent battle between Partridge and his ferocious wife, described in epic fashion. The fight was begun by Mrs. Partridge; the schoolmaster acted only in self-defense and had very much the worse of it. Rumors promptly sped and Fielding drily describes the course and reliability of the gossip: "I believe it is a true observation, that few secrets are divulged to one person only; but certainly, it would be next to a miracle that a fact of this kind [the fight] should be known to a whole parish, and not transpire any farther. And, indeed, a very few days had passed before the country, to use a common phrase, rung of the schoolmaster of Little Baddington; who was said to have beaten his wife in the most cruel manner. Nay, in some places it was reported that he had murdered her; in others, that he had broken her arms; in others, her legs: in short, there was scarce an injury which can be done to a human creature, but what Mrs. Partridge was somewhere or other affirmed to have received from her husband." Book II, Chapter V.

Captain Blifil won the hand of Bridget Allworthy because his religious sentiments seemed to be harmonious with hers. As it turns out, soon after the marriage mutual loathing takes the place of "love." Though, says Fielding, "an affection placed on the understanding is, by many wise persons, thought more durable that that which is founded on beauty, yet it happened otherwise in the present case. Nay, the understandings of this couple were their principal bone of contention, and one great cause of many quarrels which from time to time arose between them. . . ." Book II, Chapter VII.

Not only are many of Fielding's observations ironical, but also many incidents contribute to our awareness of irony. Captain Blifil, for example, "just at the very instant when his heart was exulting in meditations on the happiness which would accrue to him by Mr. Allworthy's death, he himself—died of an apoplexy." Book II, Chapter VIII.

Note: The foregoing answer makes no pretention to completeness. *Tom Jones* is so replete with irony that one would have to quote a large part of the book to give even a reasonably complete answer. The passages quoted above are designed chiefly to help the student of Fielding understand what is meant by irony.

2. Identify some of the actual people mentioned by Fielding and suggest reasons for his interest in them.

ANSWER: William Hogarth (1697-1764) was especially famous in his day for his satirical drawings. He was fond of bold effects and had a special feeling for the grotesque. Given the style and contents of *Tom Jones*, one feels that there was a spiritual kinship between the two men.

John Locke (1632-1704) was unquestionably the most influential English philosopher of his generation, and his writings continued to have a strong influence throughout the eighteenth century. Every educated man would, as a matter of course, have read Locke. Fielding might have been particularly interested in Locke because one of his most challenging books was on education, and it is clear throughout *Tom Jones* that Fielding was intensely interested in education and in educational theory.

Sir Edward Coke (1552-1634), an authority on English law, would inevitably have been read by Fielding in the course of his studies for the bar.

John Wilmot, the Second Earl of Rochester (c., 1647-1680) was one of the courtiers of Charles II, notable for his profligacy in an exceptionally profligate society. But Rochester was not only a rioter, drunkard, and lecher. He was also a wit and a talented poet. Furthermore, he became something of a legend when he made a death-bed repentance.

Fielding's mention of Rochester is so incidental that speculations on its significance are perhaps unnecessary. One would expect, however, a man of Fielding's tastes and temperament to relish Rochester's wit, and one is further prompted to think that Rochester, the celebrated penitent, almost naturally crossed Fielding's mind (if only briefly and imperceptibly) as he went on with his story of Tom's spiritual pilgrimage.

Anthony Ashley Cooper, the Third Earl of Shaftesbury (1671-1713), philosopher and man of letters, was particularly noted for his optimistic view of man. His writings did much to encourage eighteenth-century skepticism, chiefly in its Deist form. It seems clear that Square is a spokesman for some of Shaftesbury's ideas, and this fact might tend to suggest that Fielding had some reservations as to their worth. On the other hand, Fielding was not immune from the Deistic influences of his age and unquestionably would have found much in Shaftesbury with which he would have agreed. It is probable that his chief objection to Shaftesbury is that, in both his life and writings, he seems to have been too far removed from the harsh realities of life.

It may, perhaps, be worth remarking that the education of Lord Shaftesbury had been under the direction of that great educational theorist, John Locke.

Shakespeare. It almost goes without saying that Fielding mentions Shakespeare, and on more than one occasion. Both in itself and in its relation to the plot, the visit to the theater when *Hamlet* was being played (Book XVI, Chapter V) deserves close attention. The fact that the play was *Hamlet* permitted Fielding to elaborate on his recurring joke about Partridge's fear of ghosts. It also allowed him to expatiate on a subject very close to his heart and about which he knew a great deal—the theater.

David Garrick (1719-1779), the most famous actor of the eighteenth century, is represented as playing the ghost in the production of *Hamlet* attended by Tom and Partridge. Garrick was not only an actor but a manager, playwright, poet, and editor. His version of *Hamlet* was greatly admired in its time and still has great importance in the history of the staging of Shakespeare.

Homer. Writing, as he was, "a comic epic in prose," Fielding inevitably alludes to the poet who was thought to be the originator of the epic manner. (This is not the place to go into the present state of Homeric scholarship.) Not only does Fielding explicitly mention Homer, but in his frequent resort to the mock-heroic style he also imitates the mannerisms of Homer.

Many other writers are either quoted or alluded to in *Tom Jones,* but enough has been said to demonstrate that the novel cannot be dismissed as a rowdy farce. It is, among other things, an elegant and sophisticated specimen of eighteenth-century writing. Fielding obviously took for granted that at least some of his readers would be men of considerable literary education.

3. Discuss Fielding's handling of time in *Tom Jones.*

ANSWER: The plot of *Tom Jones* seems to be constructed in a straightforward chronological arrangement. The reader soon discovers, however, that the "omniscient" author is unwilling to share all of his omniscience with the reader. He tells, at any point of his story, just as much as he wishes to tell, and no more. This, of course, is his privilege. Any artist, as Fielding himself insisted, is entitled to establish the rules of the "game" that he plays with those who want to enjoy his art.

Information is communicated by Fielding in various ways. Sometimes it is by hint or indirection, as when he tells us of Bridget Allworthy's somewhat unexpected solicitude for the foundling, who ultimately is revealed to be her son. Sometimes it is by a flashback, as when he tells us something (but by no means all) of the history of Mrs. Waters, or when he tells us of Allworthy's kindness to Mrs. Miller.

The sequence of events in the main story, the story of Tom Jones in his quest of love and identity, is relatively simple, but the number of characters who intrude into Tom's story is so large that our understanding of precisely who they are and how they belong to the central story inevitably takes time.

The deliberate suppression of information (to achieve desirable ends such as suspense and surprise) is made excusable by the "omniscient" author's guileless assertion that he intends to be selective in the events that he narrates, that there will be many time-gaps in the "history" of Tom Jones. On the one hand he pretends to be telling a simple account of what happened to Tom from his birth to his reformation and marriage; on the other hand, he omits years of his hero's life from his narrative, and therefore "has to" supply incidental information about the past in various sections of the story.

Fielding's treatment of time can be examined in another way: from the point of view of how things are said as well as of what is said. As Fielding observes in the prefatory chapter to Book II, some of his chapters are very short, some very long. This is partly, of course, to achieve stylistic variety, but it also represents a subtle device for alerting us to the implications of his pose as a highly selective historian. It simultaneously alerts us and lulls us, and thus abets the author in the tricks he plays upon us. The reader is so beguiled by the structure (which must be viewed as an important part of the style) that he constantly finds himself caught off guard. Fielding plays a wicked game with his readers, and, naturally, always holds all the top cards.

Time in *Tom Jones* can be scrutinized in still another way. Necessary fundamental questions must be raised. When, for example, were the events narrated imagined to have taken place? Some answers are obvious. Garrick was already established as one of the outstanding theatrical figures of his day. There are also references in the novel to the Jacobite uprising of 1745, the dramatic and final effort of the Stuarts to regain the throne of England.

Related to Fielding's scrupulous location of his story in his own time and country is his obvious concern with unchanging human nature. He knew, as we all do, that customs change; he also knew that there are some things (however indeterminate they may prove to be) that are unchangeable in human nature; and, in a manner of speaking, he risked his artistic reputation on this conviction. Put in other terms, *Tom Jones* is both intimately related to its own time and is timeless.

4. Is Fielding unduly optimistic about the human situation?

ANSWER: Throughout *Tom Jones* the reader encounters wry comments about the observable behavior of human beings. The comments are prompted by the actions that they are credited with in the novel. By far the majority of characters are selfish, malicious, cruel, hypocritical, foolish, and stupid. It is difficult to think of Fielding as an optimist—and we know that he was skeptical of the optimistic views of Lord Shaftesbury.

If (in his personal philosophy, as opposed to his artistic strategies)

Fielding is "realistic" and recognizes that we live in a very imperfect world—and one that is likely to continue imperfect—he also refuses to take the easy way out like the pessimist and reject the world entirely. There are Blifils in the world, and strange creatures like Thwackum and Square; there are also people like Squire Allworthy and Sophia Western (the fact that Sophia is the daughter of Squire Western is one of Fielding's crowning ironies and an important clue to his outlook on life) and Mrs. Miller and, the "hero" of his great novel, Tom Jones himself.

Fielding's stance is obviously in the middle of the road. The optimism of writers like Shaftesbury he rejects; on the other hand, he refuses to deny the existence of virtue, as exemplified by Allworthy and Sophia, or as seen in exciting potentiality in Tom Jones.

Fielding is essentially level-headed and does not look at life through rose-colored glasses or through the dark glasses of despair. He seems to think of himself as a man who has rid himself of illusions, as a man who can comfortably look upon things as they are. And as he looks he sees that men are avaricious, lecherous, selfish, and, in general, deplorable; he also sees that some people are good; he further sees that other people have the seeds of goodness in them.

Considering his intimate knowledge of human viciousness and folly, it can scarcely be maintained that Fielding was an optimist. Considering, on the other hand, the holiness of the heart's affections, it can scarcely be maintained that he was a pessimist.

Fielding clearly thought of himself as a realist—but it must be understood that this term applies to his vision of life rather than to his literary technique. *Tom Jones,* as a work of art, has many virtues; realism is not one of them. Nor should realism be looked upon as an indispensable ingredient of significant art. There are many artistic strategies; realism is only one of them.

5. Discuss Fielding as a literary critic.

ANSWER: Fielding's most notable contributions to critical theory are to be found in the prefatory chapters to the "Books" of *Tom Jones*. These informal discourses are, for the most part, jocular in tone, but one can infer from them the author's serious convictions about literature. Some of the most important of these convictions are:

a) That an author has some kind of responsibility to his readers. This is, of course, a belief that Fielding shared with virtually all of his contemporaries and predecessors, and is worth mentioning only because after the eighteenth century there was a widespread feeling that authors possessed absolute rights and could and should do whatever they pleased.

b) That one of his responsibilities to his readers is that he avoid dullness. He must be selective and concentrate on the significant details that have relevance to his particular design.

c) That another of his responsibilities is to "truth." Fielding's view of truth, however, is thoroughly sophisticated. He never confuses fiction with non-truth, but he believes that the serious writer must direct his attention to things that really matter. Specifically, the writer must in one way or another faithfully depict "human nature." Here again Fielding was in agreement with most of his contemporaries.

d) That in spite of his obligation to truth the artist should not be constrained by arbitrary rules. There were critics in the eighteenth century who insisted that there were rigid rules for various kinds of writing. Fielding opposed such critics. He was far from being alone in his position, but he is an eloquent and witty spokesman for the liberal point of view.

e) That, following the precept of Aristotle, the writer should keep "within the rules of probability."

f) That excellence in writing does not proceed entirely from native abilities but must be achieved by conscious intellectual effort. Here again Fielding stands four-square with his contemporaries who, characteristically, emphasized the importance of rational judgment. Romantic writers of the late eighteenth century and the first half of the nineteenth century characteristically emphasized the importance of the emotions and rebelled against the neoclassical stress on mind.

g) That a writer is a kind of craftsman and has an obligation to learn his craft. This again seems obvious and indisputable, but later, the Romantics liked to call attention to the mystery of artistic creation and to insist upon the importance of inspiration rather than of hard work.

h) That the writer should be familiar with books but should also have a direct knowledge of life itself. Again Fielding expresses convictions by which men of his time lived. It was generally taken for granted that a gentleman should have an extensive acquaintance with literature, both ancient and modern, but should not be pedantic.

i) That it is an obligation of critics to rise above their prejudices and approach a work of art with an open mind. There were probably no more bad critics in the eighteenth century than in any other, but the dominant tendencies of neoclassical thought encouraged a special kind of critical rigidity against which the best minds of the age quite properly rebelled.

j) That a distinction should be drawn between downright plagiarism and the proper exploitation of literary tradition. This distinction is made in the first chapter of Book XII. Fielding's tone is, as usual, jocular, but the reader feels that he thinks the distinction important.

k) That literature should not only improve the minds of readers but should also educate their hearts, and encourage compassion. Implicit in this conviction is the further conviction that literature does something far more vital than supply amusement. Fielding obviously relishes his jests but he believes that even low farce can serve a serious purpose.

l) That writers should have familiarity with whatever subjects they choose to write on. All literary theorists of every age are likely to agree with this precept. Fielding does not, therefore, present it baldly or pretentiously, but expresses it in a good-humored satirical disquisition on some of the bad writers of his time.

m) That writers have an obligation to show some kind of originality. Fielding's caustic remarks on stereotyped prologues (Book XVI, Chapter I) reveal his commitment to this obvious principle.

n) Related to this principle is Fielding's belief that writers should not have resort to incredible contrivances (such as, on the ancient stage, the sudden appearance of a god—the *deus ex machina*) to advance the plot. It may be suggested that Fielding was only partially serious about this principle because *Tom Jones* abounds in unlikely coincidences. It may well be that this is really an ironical comment on the critical rigidity of Fielding's contemporaries.

SUGGESTED TOPICS FOR TERM PAPERS

INTRODUCTORY REMARKS: Careful investigation of a clearly defined problem related to *Tom Jones* will inevitably heighten a student's awareness of Fielding's art. The possibilities for research papers are limitless. Only a few obvious suggestions are made here.

Before choosing a subject, a student should examine the resources of the library or libraries available to him. Should he wish, for example, to investigate Somersetshire, he had best make sure that his library is strong on English travel books, topographical and geographical books, and county histories.

TOPICS

1) FIELDING'S USE OF DIALECT. Among his many gifts, Fielding had a remarkable ear for speech, and in *Tom Jones* he has reproduced several English dialects. One approach to this problem is to consult books on dialectal differences in England and to see how faithfully Fielding has represented these differences. Another approach is to consider the uses to which Fielding puts dialect. Does he use it exclusively for comic effect? Does he, perhaps, use it for the more careful delineation of character? Is dialect possibly helpful in his communication of his ironical view of life? Still another approach is to examine dialect in relationship to Fielding's attitude towards social differences. Is he more ready to parody the speech of servants than the speech of fashionable ladies and gentlemen?

2) FIELDING AND THE THEATER. The student might well begin by collecting all references to the theater in *Tom Jones*. He could then do one or more of several interesting things: he could make a study of eighteenth-century London theaters and consider the value of the evidence offered by Fielding. He could examine Fielding's plays and speculate on the value of his experience as dramatist to him when he turned his hand to novels. He could concentrate his attention on a very specific subject—eighteenth-century prologues, for example. Or he could see what he could find out about David Garrick. Or about eighteenth-century productions of Shakespeare—or even about eighteenth-century versions of *Hamlet*.

3) THE DEBATES OF THWACKUM AND SQUARE. Since it is clear that Thwackum and Square are, in a manner of speaking, antagonists of the narrator of *Tom Jones*, an attentive reader might gain insights into Fielding's attitude toward such things as philos-

ophy, religion, and education through a careful analysis of the opinions of the optimistic Square and the rigorist Thwackum. Or one could analyze the various ways in which these two characters are used to further the main plot of the novel. Is there any distinction between Fielding's attitudes toward these two adversaries?

4) FIELDING AS HISTORIAN. Students whose library resources are meager can attack this problem. Fielding himself says that he is an "historian." Why? Is he serious in his claim or jocular? What does he think about history? To what kinds of writing does he oppose his historical kind? What is Fielding's view of the artist's responsibility to truth? What kind of historical writing does he satirize? With how much justice?

5) FIELDING AND ROMANCE. Related to Topic 4 is the problem of Fielding's attitude toward romance. Investigation of this problem should deepen a student's understanding of neoclassical attitudes on the limits of the writer's imagination, the relevance of literature to life, the nature of the classical tradition, and the respective merits of the ancients and moderns. A student choosing this topic should first collect all of Fielding's remarks on romance, organize them into categories, and then study them against the literary, social, and intellectual tendencies of the eighteenth century.

6) THE RELIGIOUS CLIMATE OF EIGHTEENTH-CENTURY ENGLAND. There are obviously many ways to approach this vast subject. One might, for example, confine one's attention to the Established Church. Even in doing this a student would be wise if he further narrowed his subject to any one of several possible subjects: the education of the clergy, the living conditions of the clergy—in the country, in towns, in cities—, the popularity of sermon literature, or the hierarchical structure of the English Church, to name but a few possibilities. Or a student might conceivably be interested in studying some of the dissenting sects such as the Methodists and the Quakers. Deism could profitably be studied.

7) THE SERVANT PROBLEM IN THE EIGHTEENTH CENTURY. How well were they paid? How were they treated? How did they regard themselves? How were they recruited? List the servants in *Tom Jones* and study Fieldings representation of them.

8) SPORT IN THE EIGHTEENTH CENTURY. The English passion for fox-hunting is, of course, a subject of obvious importance. Some students might find it interesting to investigate the game-laws of the century. Some might want to see if and how sports were the*n* organized. What other sports were widely popular? What were the sports chiefly enjoyed by the gentry? By the common people?

Does Fielding have a discernible attitude towards sport? How is sport used in the development of the "meaning" of *Tom Jones?*

9) EDUCATION IN THE EIGHTEENTH CENTURY. Some students might want to investigate village schools, others the great "public schools," and still others the universities. Some students might want to explore educational theory—for example, the ideas of John Locke. Some are likely to be especially interested in what Fielding has to say about education. What, in general, was studied in eighteenth-century English schools? In the universities?

10) THE GRAND TOUR. Among the privileged, an extended tour of the Continent was thought to be an essential part of a young Englishman's education. Where did they go? What did they do? What good did it do them? A student might profitably follow in the footsteps of any one of a number of prominent Englishmen who made the Grand Tour—Boswell, Gray, Walpole, to name but a few.

11) THE LICENSING ACT OF 1737. This was the restrictive act that ended Fielding's career as dramatist. Why was it passed? Was Sir Robert Walpole as reprehensible a character as his enemies made him out to be? What were Fielding's political views? Do any of them appear in *Tom Jones?*

12) FIELDING ON LOVE. Many subjects are discussed at length in *Tom Jones,* but surely the central subject is love. A reader would almost certainly derive a fuller understanding of this challenging novel from a disciplined analysis of Fielding's remarks, both incidental and sustained, on love. The subject is so large and Fielding's comments so extensive that it would be advisable to select a manageable sub-topic such as marriage, benevolence, love-letters, or better, an even more rigidly controlled subject.

13) FIELDING'S FAMILIARITY WITH LITERATURE. The attentive reader of *Tom Jones* cannot but be impressed by the enormous range of Fielding's reading. The novel is so unremittingly and irresistibly funny that a careless reader can fail to notice how "literary" (in the best sense of that often abused word) it is. The examination of the literary allusions in *Tom Jones* is much too demanding a task for an apprentice scholar, and the student should therefore confine his attention to a limited area. Some suggestions:

REFERENCES TO HOMER
REFERENCES TO ENGLISH AUTHORS
REFERENCES TO FRENCH AUTHORS
LATIN QUOTATIONS
THE USES OF QUOTATIONS FOR IRONICAL PURPOSES

14) FIELDING AND RICHARDSON. There are any number of ways of approaching this problem. Some students might like to consult Boswell's *Life of Johnson,* which records Johnson's opinions of the respective merits of Fielding and Richardson (he preferred Richardson), and consider the merits of these opinions. Others might like to read *Shamela* and *Joseph Andrews* in their relationship to Richardson's *Pamela.* Others might want to examine the places of Richardson and Fielding in the history of the English novel. Still others, interested in the extraordinary spread of sentimentalism in the eighteenth century, will readily observe that Fielding is inclined to laugh at the kind of sentimentalism to be found in Richardson's novels, and may further observe that Fielding, for all of his satire at the expense of Richardson and for all of his earthiness and common-sense, is not totally immune to the effects of the contemporary cult of feeling.

16) FIELDING'S LONDON. *Tom Jones* can be described as a panoramic view of eighteenth-century England. Some of the action takes place in the country, some in "the town," i.e., London. Much of what Fielding says is perfectly lucid and self-explanatory, but his London was strikingly different from any cities we are acquainted with today. A student's appreciation of *Tom Jones* will inevitably be enhanced if he makes a systematic study of various features of eighteenth-century London. Some suggested topics:

CLUB LIFE
FASHIONABLE AMUSEMENTS
SHOPS
MODES OF TRANSPORTATION
CHARITABLE INSTITUTIONS
THE POLICE
DOMESTIC ARCHITECTURE
CHURCHES AND CHAPELS
INNS AND HOSTELRIES
HEALTH MEASURES
APPRENTICES
ATTITUDES TOWARD THE MONARCHY

17) THE ENGLISH LANGUAGE IN THE EIGHTEENTH CENTURY. It is a well-known fact that language patterns change, at varying rates of speed in response to varying historical situations. Although travel and media of communication such as radio and television have tended to level out many differences between English and American speech, many differences nevertheless remain. And in both England and America there is a considerable amount of dialectal variety in spite of all levelling influences.

Although readers of Fielding need not expect excessive difficulties because of the differences between his language and the language now in common use, it should be pointed out that a fair proportion of words used in *Tom Jones* are no longer current. Readers ought, therefore, to find it entertaining and enlightening to keep a list of unfamiliar words, with their eighteenth-century meanings.

A few examples:

The very first sentence of *Tom Jones* reads: "An author ought to consider himself, not as a gentleman who gives a private or eleemosynary treat, but rather as one who keeps a public ordinary, at which all persons are welcome for their money." Some readers may boggle at the "learned" word, "eleemosynary" ("charitable"), as they may boggle at many other deliberately pretentious words that Fielding uses to establish his mock-heroic tone. Other readers may need to be told that the word "gentleman" had a more precise meaning in Fielding's day than it has today: it described a caste and connoted birth, breeding, and privilege. Almost all modern readers, however, will need to be instructed on the meaning of "public ordinary." This was the usual eighteenth-century term for what we call a restaurant. Occasionally we encounter in Fielding, and, indeed, in other eighteenth-century authors, the word "enthusiasm." The word today has no special sinister undertones, but in Fielding's day it was, at least in some circles, almost synonymous with lunacy. "Enthusiasm" was at variance with "common-sense." It also stood for a characteristic of the evangelical Methodists—and men of Fielding's stamp detested the Methodists. They thought of the Methodist preoccupation with piety either as an affectation or as something socially unacceptable.

Tom's education, it will be recalled, was entrusted to Thwackum. Fielding amusingly tells us that Thwackum's "meditations were full of birch.'" The corporal punishment of schoolchildren, at least in the United States, has largely gone out of fashion, so Fielding's phrase may convey little meaning to American readers of *Tom Jones*. In the eighteenth century, however, children were unmercifully beaten, not only for misconduct but for failure to perform, without error, school assignments. Not everyone in the century was happy about the prevailing educational methods. Pope in his *Dunciad* excoriates the brutality of the system, and it is clear that Fielding's portrait of Square is a denunciation of it and a plea for more humane attitudes toward children. "Birch," then, is not simply a word to be defined, but also a word to be seen in its full historical perspective—as evidence of Fielding's benevolence and humanitarianism, as part of eighteenth century sentimentalism, as an implicit proposal for educational reform. (Suggestion: Look into John Locke's educational theories.)

SELECTED BIBLIOGRAPHY

BIOGRAPHY

Cross, W. L. *The History of Henry Fielding,* 3 vols., 1918. Although written many years ago, this remains an indispensable work for the student of Fielding. It is not only indispensable; it is delightful. Wilbur L. Cross (1862-1948) was an energetic and meticulous scholar, but he lived in no ivory tower. He was by temperament peculiarly equipped for appreciation of Fielding's range of interests and zest for living.

Dudden, F. Homes. *Henry Fielding: His Life, Works, and Times,* 2 vols., 1952. This is an excellent book. It does not offer enough new material to make it, rather than Cross's book, the standard biography, but it does represent a fresh re-working of the evidence and is continually illuminating.

CRITICAL STUDIES: GENERAL

Digeon, A. *The Novels of Fielding,* 1925. Originally published in French in 1923, this contribution to Fielding studies was so obviously important as to justify translation into English.

Blanchard, F. T. *Fielding the Novelist,* 1926.

Thornbury, Ethel M. *Henry Fielding's Theory of the Comic Prose Epic,* 1931. This is a thoroughly admirable exploration of Fielding's own notions of what he was doing in *Joseph Andrews* and *Tom Jones.* Students investigating such subjects as Fielding's literary criticism or his reading or his attitude toward the classics or his mocking spirit will do well to consult this book.

Bissell, Frederic O. *Fielding's Theory of the Novel,* 1933. This usefully supplements Miss Thornbury's study of a particular aspect of Fielding's literary theory.

Murry, John Middleton. "In Defense of Fielding," *Unprofessional Essays,* 1956. A first-rate English journalist and critic here attempts a re-appraisal of Fielding and does much to sharpen our perceptions of the values in Fielding's writings.

CRITICAL STUDIES: INDIVIDUAL WORKS

Battestin, Martin C. *The Moral Basis of Fielding's Art: a Study of*

"Joseph Andrews," 1959. This ranks among the most important of the comparatively recent studies of Fielding, and is particularly good in its insistence on the fundamental seriousness of the novelist. Any reader can see that Fielding is good-humored and amusing; it takes a little application to arrive at an understanding that he believed in the ultimate importance of literature in the heightening of man's understanding of his basic responsibilities.

McKillop, A. D. "Some Recent Views of *Tom Jones," College English,* October 1959, pp. 17-22.

Woods, Charles B. "Fielding and the Authorship of *Shamela," Philological Quarterly,* July 1946, pp. 248-272.

BACKGROUND STUDIES

Baugh, A. C. ed., *A Literary History of England,* 1948. Generally considered to be the best one-volume history of English literature. The chapters on the Restoration and the eighteenth century were prepared by George Sherburn, widely looked upon as one of the greatest of recent students of the English eighteenth century. This is a book that a student may use with confidence.

Moore, C. A. *Backgrounds of English Literature, 1700-1760,* 1953.

Humphreys, A. R. *The Augustan World,* 1954.

Carritt, E. F. *A Calendar of British Taste,* 1949.

Swedenberg, H. T. Jr. *The Theory of the Epic in England, 1650-1800,* 1944. Since Fielding partly, but only partly, in jest, related his work to the classical epic, it is well for the student to have some awareness of the attitudes toward the epic that prevailed in eighteenth-century England. This has become one of the accepted major contributions toward our understanding of these attitudes.

MacLean, Kenneth, *John Locke and English Literature of the Eighteenth Century,* 1936.

Jack, Ian. *Augustan Satire,* 1952.

Highet, Gilbert. *The Classical Tradition,* 1949.

Timbs, John. *Clubs and Club Life in London,* 1872.

Wheatley, H. P. and Cunningham, P. *London, Past and Present,* 1891.

George, M. D. *English Social Life,* 1923. *London Life,* 1925.

Turberville, A. S. *English Men and Manners in the Eighteenth Century,* 1926 (now available in paperback). Few books can be much more useful than this to the student who is beginning to make an acquaintance with the English eighteenth century. It is, necessarily, sketchy, but it is wide-ranging, informative, and lively.

Perkins, M. H. *The Servant Problem and the Servant in English Literature,* 1928. The study of literature and the study of sociology should not be confused, but Fielding, as has been remarked earlier in this book, was a keen observer and critic of manners. He obviously was interested in the "servant problem."

Hartley, D. and Elliot, M. M. *Life and Work of the People of England: Eighteenth Century,* 1931.

Mason, J. E. *Gentlefolk in the Making,* 1934.

Bayne-Powell, Rosamond. *English Country Life in the Eighteenth Century,* 1935. *Eighteenth-Century London Life,* 1937. Miss Bayne-Powell has established herself as a consistently interesting social historian. Students of writers like Fielding will find her books immensely helpful.

Whitely, J. H. *Wesley's England,* 1938. Although one cannot ignore the importance of any one of the dissenting sects, the Methodist movement seems to have been one of the most permanently significant events in English religious history. Fielding was far from being sympathetic with the zealous Methodists, but he could scarcely ignore them in his books, and the student is well advised to be aware of the place of Methodism in English religious, social, and political history.

Kirby, Paul. *The Grand Tour in Italy,* 1952.

A CONCLUDING NOTE

It should be obvious that even a selective bibliography of studies of the English eighteenth century could extend to hundreds of pages. The student should realize that the titles listed here are meant to increase his consciousness of the wealth of scholarship that is at his disposal and that can, if properly used, be a permanent source of pleasure.

Fielding did not write his books so that centuries later they might become problems to be solved in a classroom. He wrote them: a) to entertain his contemporaries; b) to challenge his contemporaries—to make them think about the actualities behind the facade of fashionable life, about the relationship between religious dogma and actual behavior, about selfishness and the essential nature of charity, about the human situation. He is an important author, but he has a most agreeable unconsciousness of his importance.

That Fielding is a casual, companionable, undemanding author, however, should not blind the reader to pertinent facts. Fielding wrote about a society that has disappeared. He wrote in a style that belongs to another world than that we know. He was exercised about issues that no longer have special relevance.

It follows from this that a reader's enjoyment will be increased if he takes the most obvious steps to acquaint himself with Fielding's England. The steps, naturally, have to be one after another. The acquisition of information takes time. But it should be enjoyable. If a student, let us say, can enjoy a cinematic representation of an eighteenth-century English country inn, he also ought to be able to enjoy books and articles that increase his familiarity with such an inn. If a student likes to see a cinematic representation of an eighteenth-century London bargeman, why should he not want to know about such things as a bargeman's wages, habits, prospects?

Tom Jones is a warm, compassionate, witty, wise, tonic book. It should not be disfigured, misused, or in any way molested by academicians. But it is so enjoyable, so good, so useful, that any student who reads habitually because he finds reading absolutely necessary to his development—spiritual, intellectual, social—will do the necessary homework.

CONCLUSION: Fielding's position in the history of English literature is beyond question: he is one of our first great novelists, and he is among the most sophisticated commenters on the technical problems that are confronted by the creative artist. *Tom Jones,* however, is not read today because it is something that belongs to history; it is read because it has never lost its relevance. A vast chasm exists between the eighteenth century and the twentieth century; *Tom Jones* bridges the chasm. We learn from the books of the past. Homer still teaches us; Virgil, Ovid, Juvenal still teach us; Fielding still teaches us. Anyone who reads *Tom Jones* without a conciousness of being in the presence of genius ought to make a serious examination of his conscience.

NOTES

NOTES

NOTES

NOTES

NOTES

NOTES

NOTES

NOTES

NOTES

NOTES

NOTES

NOTES

NOTES

NOTES

NOTES